TAKEOVER

To Betty Baker

Takeover

Sam Volard

Gower

Published by
Gower Publishing Limited
Gower House
Croft Road
Aldershot
Hampshire GU11 3HR
England

Gower
Old Post Road
Brookfield
Vermont 05036
USA

British Library Cataloguing in Publication Data
Volard, Sam V.
Takeover
1. Consolidation and merger of corporations 2. Consolidation and merger of corporations – Fiction
I. Title
338.8′3

ISBN 0 566 07728 0

Library of Congress Cataloging-in-Publication Data
Volard, Sam V., 1930–
Takeover / Sam V. Volard.
p. cm.
ISBN 0–566–07728–0 (cloth)
1. Consolidation and merger of corporations—Fiction. I. Title.
PR9619.3.V58T35 1997
823—dc21 96–32171
CIP

Typeset in 11 on 14pt Goudy by Intype London Ltd and printed in Great Britain at the University Press, Cambridge.

Contents

Preface vii
Acknowledgements ix

Part I Rumours
1 6.00 p.m., Tuesday, 24 December 3
2 11.30 a.m., Saturday, 28 December 13
3 10.30 p.m., Tuesday, 31 December 32

Part II Announcements
4 7.00 a.m., Thursday, 2 January 41
5 4.00 p.m., Thursday, 2 January 59
6 7.00 a.m., Friday, 3 January 62
7 4.00 p.m., Friday, 3 January 69
8 3.30 p.m., Sunday, 5 January 74

Part III Changes at the top
9 10.00 a.m., Monday, 6 January 85
10 3.00 p.m., Friday, 10 January 94
11 11.45 a.m., Wednesday, 15 January 102

12 3.00 p.m., Friday, 17 January 109
13 2.30 p.m., Sunday, 26 January 122

Part IV Changes everywhere
14 3.00 p.m., Friday, 1 February 133
15 1.00 p.m., Tuesday, 19 February 141
16 8.15 p.m., Friday, 1 March 145
17 10.45 p.m., Saturday, 2 March 154
18 11.00 a.m., Monday, 16 March 162

Part V A new beginning
19 11.45 a.m., Monday, 18 May 173
20 1.00 p.m., Tuesday, 22 July 183
21 10.30 p.m., Friday, 7 November 193
22 3.50 p.m., Thursday, 11 December 202
23 9.30 a.m., Sunday, 28 December 217
Commentary 227

Preface

Company takeovers have become commonplace events in an international business environment where competitive realignments are important determinants of corporate policy. There is a great deal to commend this "sorting out" activity: better products are created, prices are kept down, service is improved. Nonetheless, such events do not occur without considerable disruption, even trauma, to the "people" side of enterprise as the affected workforces are reorganized to better achieve anticipated benefits. It is this issue which is the focus of my business novel.

It is a work of fiction and can be read for enjoyment. However, it is also very much a learning tool. It provides the reader with insights into the complex and multifaceted characteristics of takeovers. These insights are especially important since the impact on employees who are being taken over is generally not well understood, nor is the process by which they can be successfully assimilated into an alien, often hostile, organizational environment. This book addresses these critical issues and the plot develops against the background of two interdependent business imperatives: devising a set of *guiding concepts and shared values* which are embraced by employees in order to achieve corporate objectives, and implementing a change programme whose purpose is to create a *high involvement workforce*.

The novel covers a period of one year, from a week or so before the takeover is consummated to the stage when it is fully integrated into the new owner's operations. It describes the effect of the takeover on the employees through the eyes of four long-term managers. The acquisition is a free-standing division in the human ethical prescription drug business. The former parent company is an international corporation concerned almost exclusively with the research, development and marketing of veterinary pharmaceuticals, biologicals and supplies. The new proprietor, also a large international corporation, is predominantly in human ethical over-the-counter drugs, with a need to reorganize its existing prescription drug operations into a more viable and profitable business entity.

The text consists of five parts, each dealing with an identifiable phase of the takeover, and twenty-three chapters, each describing a specific episode. Each chapter presents one or more *learning points* that provide useful perspectives on takeovers. At the end of the text there is a chapter-by-chapter analysis that examines these learning points. I would encourage the reader to study them as part of the total intellectual experience.

Sam Volard

Acknowledgements

There are four people who made this book possible:

My wife, Lizzie (Betty Baker) in Richmond, Virginia, who provided me with the love and support to try my hand at writing fiction, after decades of playing the academic "publish or perish" game.

Dr Bruce Christie, veterinary pathologist extraordinaire, formerly with Dupont Pharmaceutical in Wilmington, Delaware, who suggested I place the story in that industry, and explained many of its little known secrets and technicalities.

My daughter-in-law, Katie, in Brisbane, Australia, who always seemed to have the time to edit sections as I completed them. Although I consider myself a reasonably "tidy" writer, she almost always found mistakes and suggested changes here and there that made all the difference to the quality of the final manuscript.

Last but by no means least, Malcolm Stern, Editorial Director, Gower Publishing, without whose encouragement and guidance this book would never have been written. I owe him a lot!

Part I
Rumours

Chapter 1

6.00 p.m., Tuesday, 24 December

Brian Curtis closed down his computer with a flourish. This would have to do for the day – in fact, for the year. Another year gone by, another division Christmas party waiting for him in the atrium, another week's holiday by the sea coming up. He stretched and yawned loudly. He was certainly looking forward to that week away because it would be their first time ever with no children. He smiled. Pretty shrewd these youngsters, presenting such a united front. They had apparently held a secret meeting and decided they were too grown up to continue sharing bedrooms with their parents. They wanted to stay at home and do things with their friends over that Christmas week instead. At a recent combined family barbecue, it had been agreed, to joyful cheers and kisses, that they could stay at home and look after themselves and their pets. It was very clearly understood that the older ones would make sure the younger ones behaved, they would keep everything neat and tidy, they would all be models of discretion and decorum . . . or there would be hell to pay when their parents returned home!

Among themselves, of course, the parents agreed it would be

bliss not having them underfoot, pushing, fighting, screaming, running everywhere, taking forever in the bathrooms, out on the beach, always getting wet. And then coming back into the house shivering, visions of pneumonia in the worried eyes of the mothers, frustration on the faces of the fathers. How long had they done this, he asked himself, pushing back his desk chair? This would be the seventh year. Four couples, six children – well, three families, and Britt Berghoff with some young stud in tow and no children.

He remembered that Sunday seven years ago so clearly, driving on the beach road in his old Ford estate. Gretl was in the passenger seat, Britt, no man in tow for a change, in the back, and Kimmy nestled up to Britt's large bosom, sucking her thumb as she typically did when she was bored. The sky was grey and forbidding, the waves crashing loudly on the long shoreline. Both women yelled at the same time for him to stop and back the car. They came to a standstill in front of a large brown and white billboard in the scraggly front garden of this enormous old house backing onto the sea.

"Can you imagine, Britt?" Gretl whispered with awe. They read the billboard together, their voices rising and falling with each new detail.

> Four bedrooms with four full en suite bathrooms, play-room complete with billiard table and jacuzzi: large sundeck with built-in barbecue, huge living room with fireplace, fully equipped kitchen, fully furnished, every service provided. Bring your food and drinks and move right in. Children and pets welcome. Available for one week between Christmas and New Year.

They paused to catch their breath. And then they sat back, mouths agape, as the possibilities presented themselves.

Britt was first to break the silence. "What kind of rent do you think they want?" she asked Gretl in a Germanic accent she had never managed to shed.

He remembered telling them it would be too much and had let the car roll forward, accompanied by yells to stop. "Let's go and ask, darling. It can't hurt to ask," Gretl had told him archly, in that pleading voice he could never resist.

Britt tapped him firmly on the shoulder. "Dr Curtis, I respectfully order you to drive us this minute to the real estate agent. I will accept only a 'yes' for an answer," she had declared in a monotone.

Gretl and he had laughed uproariously at the drollness of that command and Kimmy had joined them by screeching and clapping her hands. And then they were at the real estate agency, and it all became possible when they shared the rent between four couples. And that's what they had done for that week between Christmas and New Year, and ever since – the same four couples going away together to the same wonderful old beach house on the same desolate stretch of coast, complete with children and dogs. No cats, please! All so predictable, so secure, the way life ought to be for professional middle managers on generous salaries.

He looked round his office, lined with filing cabinets and crowded bookcases, untidy but comfortable, like an old shoe. He had always liked returning to his office. There was something reassuring about having such a place to call his very own, something on which he had firmly and indelibly imprinted his style and personality, something no one, it seemed, would ever take away from him. In fact, they had all done quite well in the small Human Ethicals Division of AgriBus International. "Yes," he reflected, looking around him with satisfaction. "They've been good years."

He had occasionally secretly acknowledged to himself how uneasily their division fitted into a very large corporation whose almost exclusive focus was the research, development and marketing of veterinary pharmaceuticals, biologicals and supplies. There was some synergy in the sharing of technology, but he knew AgriBus could shrug them off without noticing the difference. He was sure these thoughts must have crossed the minds of some of the directors. Nonetheless, the corporation continued to support human ethicals in the hope that they would one day discover a drug which would earn them a zillion. More importantly, it gave the corporation a certain air of respectability. They were able to say that they were interested in people and not just animals, but without having to detail the extent of that interest, which in the scheme of AgriBus affairs was minuscule.

He sensed rather than saw Britt standing at his shoulder. She had an uncanny way of opening doors in total silence and gliding noiselessly over the ground, in spite of her generous proportions. "Hello, Beebee," he greeted her with an easy familiarity born of years of working and socializing with her. "Don't tell me the party's over?" he asked, looking quickly at his wristwatch.

She massaged his shoulders gently, digging in her strong fingers where the tension points had built up. "You work too hard, my Brian. Do you think Gretl would mind very much if we made love on the floor of your office? It is so boring at the party and I am tired of drinking lemonade. I have to drive myself home tonight and the police will be out in force. I do not need a 'Drinking under the Influence' ticket on Christmas Eve, do you think, my beautiful one?"

Brian Curtis stood and gave her a kiss on the cheek. "Another time, another life, and you would have trouble keeping my hands from running all over your sexy body. Yes, my handsome one, Gretl would take great exception to us having a roll on the carpet. It would also be the end of a beautiful friendship. Why don't you leave your car here and I'll run you home. Anyway, where is young Ron tonight? Why isn't he picking you up?"

"Young Ron, as you say, is off with his boyfriends drinking, he tells me. He will be home sometime before dawn, he tells me. Young Ron will not last much longer, I am thinking. He continues with me for the moment only because he has good manners and I need him at the beach next week."

"That's not quite true, Beebee, and you know it. He's a personable young man and he keeps you very happy, we all know. And, yes, he has excellent manners and we all quite like him. He's also an excellent mechanic, which is very useful. Anyway, think about my taking you home, in which case you can drink as much as you like. Now, let's join the party. I was just about to close up shop when you started massaging my back, which, incidentally, was exactly what I needed, thank you."

He started for the door and realized that Britt was not following him. He stopped in his tracks. "Is something wrong, Britt?" he asked her, coming back to where she was still standing.

"I do not know, Brian," she replied. "Maybe there is. Have you heard the rumour about the division being sold to Helm & Hathaway?"

"This place is always full of rumours, Britt. You should know that by now. Who's getting stabbed in the back, who's dating who, who's going to be promoted? But the division being sold off? This is news to me. Where did you hear it and, more importantly, from whom?"

"A secretary from Head Office who came to our party with one of our salesmen. She says she saw the legal documents confirming the sale to H & H. She is quite tiddly, you know, so it is hard to believe her. But what will happen to us if it is true? You hear terrible stories about takeovers and what they do to employees."

"H & H? You're talking about a company that's twice as large as AgriBus, all in human ethical drugs. Why would they be interested in our little division? We have a stream of very promising drugs coming through, that's true, but they're some years away from being on the market. And most of what we already have out there is about due to become generic. These are clearly not incentives for buying us up. Anyway, I can't imagine AgriBus selling us off after putting millions into giving us some of the best R&D facilities in the industry. Apart from which, we pay our way, thank you. Not quite up to the ROI of the company's policy, but enough. I wouldn't worry about it too much, Beebee. A silly rumour, that's all it is. Now let's go and join the party." He seized her firmly by the elbow and led her out of his office, locking the door. And they walked arm in arm down the passage to the gallery overlooking the atrium.

Brian Curtis had always thought the passages were well insulated from noise. Consequently, he didn't hear anything until they were almost on the gallery. The scene that greeted him resembled a Bruegel painting: tables loaded with food and drink distributed strategically along the walls of the gallery; innumerable small groups of people, drinks in hand, scattered along the gallery talking animatedly with each other; a three-piece band on the floor below, behind the long reception desk. They were playing "Lady in Red", one of his favourites. Couples were dancing and laughing gaily around the hexagonal fountain. The water, cascading down the tiered sides into a mini rainforest, somehow intensified the hubbub of the hundreds of raised voices. It was all very reassuring and clearly didn't reflect any level of anxiety, which would certainly have been evident had the rumour been true.

Above the gallery on which they were standing, the glass roof of the atrium disappeared in the darkness overhead. The gallery itself swept majestically around the hexagonal sides of the atrium, broken only by a grand staircase directly opposite the entrance to the building. The architect had done a fine job – except for that entrance. It reminded him of the entrances to any number of large hotels in any number of cities, with their automated revolving doors and floor-to-ceiling plate glass windows on either side. Somehow, this beautiful building deserved something better than a pedestrian, if functional, entrance. But otherwise, the total effect was brilliant and captured the special kind of work they did. The interior walls of the atrium's six stories resembled the inside of a beehive, the staggered vertical and horizontal lines of windows accentuated by the glass lifts on either side which climbed delicately up the walls. In addition, each floor was identified by Star Wars-like hexagonal doors that slid pneumatically apart when a lift came to a standstill before them.

With Britt Berghoff at his side, he stopped at the balustrade and looked comfortably on this scene. He had seen it on Christmas Eve for the past eleven years, ever since the highly specialized building had been commissioned as the state-of-the-art example of what a human ethicals R&D facility should be. Each year, the AgriBus directors rewarded the four hundred or so employees of the division with this magnificent breakup party, immediately after the distribution of the generous yearly bonus. The high-class HED, as it was derisively called by the other employees of the predominantly veterinary organization, had clearly assumed a favoured place in the scheme of things, but had yet to produce the wonder drug which would justify Agri-Bus's considerable investment. And this is what worried Brian Curtis when he very occasionally discarded his scientist's hat and tried to think like a businessman. On reflection, a takeover by Helm & Hathaway wasn't such an unlikely event after all.

His thoughts were interrupted by a sharp jab in the side. "Here is trouble," Britt announced, smiling wickedly. "Let us give him something to talk about," and she curled one leg around his leg and began to nibble his earlobe.

"Aha! Brian. I see our sexy Berghoff has finally broken down your defences, you lucky man. And she your wife's best friend. Very naughty, *non!*" Armand Hernier declared jovially, his double chin and enormous stomach bobbing up and down as he approached them.

Britt straightened herself primly, smoothing down her silk dress. "*Mein Gott*, Brian, we are discovered in flagrante delicto, and by a Frenchman, no less. What an indignity," she commented in her most Germanic accent.

"All right, you two. Get it all out of your system tonight. It will be dreadful to have you carrying on this way right through the week at the beach." He separated himself from Britt and put his arm around Armand Hernier's fat shoulders. "Have you been giving all the beautiful women a hard time, *mon ami?*" he inquired.

"Impossible. All I can give women is a soft time. There is not a hard spot in the whole of my body, as you can see. Well, only on special occasions. Is that not so, my German sausage?" he asked Britt who was still pretending to ignore him, but with a big smile on her face.

Brian looked at these two very close friends, so unlike in their appearance and approach to life and work, and yet with great affection for each other. Britt Berghoff, a German immigrant and orphan who had raised herself up by the bootstraps to become a highly qualified and respected toxicologist. Armand Hernier, a French medicinal chemist who had come into the corporation as a consultant and had decided to stay. Unlike Britt, Armand had been born into a life of ease and plenty, the youngest son of wealthy landowners in Brittany. Brian loved them both dearly, if it was possible to love two people who were so dissimilar.

"You know, it will be good to get away from all this," and he waved his free arm at the party scene around them. "I can't remember when I've looked forward to being at the beach house more. And now, it's definitely time for a drink." He gave Armand Hernier a hug and, his other arm around Britt Berghoff's shoulders, walked them towards the nearest table where a wide variety of drinks were laid out on a serve-yourself basis.

As they helped themselves to drinks, Armand remarked casually, "I suppose you know, *mon* Brian, this may be the last Christmas Eve party we may enjoy together, the three musketeers and D'Artagnan."

"Not you too, Armand. I suppose you're referring to the rumour that our division is being taken over by H & H. Nothing is impossible. But if it happens, I'm sure people like us will be safe. Hell, I don't have to tell you how often I've been approached by headhunters to move from AgriBus. And that's even more true of both of you. Specialists with our skills and experience are not easy to find. So, let's forget it. There'll be many other Christmas Eve parties, whatever happens. Right now, all I want to think about is being at the beach house, sitting in the jacuzzi with Gretl and soaking up the bubbles. You can make sure my wine glass is always full, Armand, and you can massage my neck muscles, Beebee. And my darling Gretl can caress me wherever she wants. That would be as close to heaven as I could wish to be."

"Did I hear someone mention heaven?" Tony Johns, tall, thin and ungainly, long grey hair falling limply over a wide forehead, stumbled awkwardly between Armand and Britt, the red wine in his glass spilling onto the carpet. "If I didn't know better, you lecherous pair, I could get quite jealous."

"You would need to sober up first, my friendly legal eagle," Armand retorted, his jowls rising and falling as he stepped nimbly back to avoid the spilled drink.

Britt also retreated. "Tony. Be careful. This dress has just come back from the cleaners." She turned to Brian Curtis. "Control him, Brian."

Tony Johns, the division's director of regulatory affairs, grinned sheepishly. "Sorry, you two. Didn't mean to make a nuisance of myself. I suppose I've had a bit too much to drink. No worries. Gloria promised to pick me up when I was ready. Time I gave her a call." And he began to back away from the threesome.

"No you don't, Tony," Brian said quickly as he grabbed his arm. "I haven't had a drink yet, let alone one with you included to wish us all a happy Christmas. Don't worry about them. They're just sober and bitchy because they have to drive themselves home." He raised his glass of white wine and looked at his friends. "To the four of us. All for one, and one for all! A merry Christmas, and may we all stay drunk for a week, starting tomorrow."

Tony raised his glass and drained it in one gulp. "I may need to remain drunk for the year if the rumour is true. I mean, how many regulatory affairs directors can Helm & Hathaway possibly need?"

Britt immediately reached over and gave him a big kiss on the cheek. "Nothing is going to happen to any of us. It is just a stupid story from the mouth of a stupid girl. No one is taking her seriously, as you can see." She gestured at the thinning crowd of revellers on both levels. "Next year, we will all be back exactly here, celebrating Christmas once again."

Armand also reached over and patted Tony on the back. "Britt is perfectly correct. It is nonsense, *absolument*."

"I hope you people are right. What do you think, Brian?" Tony asked, facing Brian who was slowly sipping his white wine.

Brian Curtis made a face. "Who knows, Tony. Personally, I agree with Armand and Britt. It doesn't make much sense for H & H to want to take us over. Anyway, this is Christmas Eve. We'll have plenty of time to talk about the pros and cons of takeovers during the week at the beach. Not that I want to spend any time talking about a rumour, but it would be interesting to explore the subject over a few bottles of wine. I know our ladies will have a lot to say about it. In the meantime, let's enjoy the party, what's left of it. Who's for a dance around the fountain?"

"Good idea, Brian," Tony replied, immediately cheering up. "A quick spin for me, then I'd better call Gloria. Beebee, what do you say?" and he took Britt by the arm and led the way to the grand staircase, the other two following closely behind, looking for any available dancing partners on the gallery or in the reception area below.

Chapter 2

11.30 a.m., Saturday, 28 December

Armand and Michelle came quickly through the front door of the beach house, shutting the door behind them to keep the cold wind out. They dropped the large number of plastic bags containing the groceries onto the floor and took off their coats, which they threw carelessly over the back of a chair.

"Allo, everyone," Michelle called out. "We are back." They paused in the middle of the huge living-cum-dining room, waiting for a reply, but none came.

"*Ils sont drôles, tu sais*," Armand told her with a shrug. "They are probably in the jacuzzi again. I shall go and see," and he headed for the stairs leading to the basement that stretched the entire length and breadth of the house. He peered into the gloom of the furthest corner, but there was no one in the jacuzzi. It gurgled noisily at him as he approached to make sure that it was empty. They had played that trick on him the day they had arrived at the beach house and he was not going to be caught again. He had spent half an hour walking all over the house and on the beach looking for them and had finally discovered they had been hiding all along in the spa, including his own wife, Michelle, laughing their heads off as they heard him stomping about.

So, if not in the spa, where were they? Well, he decided, he would not give them the satisfaction of looking. He went upstairs again and gave Michelle a hand putting away the groceries, muttering all the time under his breath at their lack of consideration.

Some ten minutes later, just as he and Michelle had finished tidying the kitchen, he heard the others returning through the back door leading to the sundeck and the beach. Michelle called out, "We are here."

The three couples trooped into the kitchen, discarding their coats on the nearest chairs on the way. Armand ignored them and continued putting away the last of the cutlery in the drawer with exaggerated gestures. The signs were unmistakable: Armand was still in a Gallic bad mood. They looked at Michelle who grimaced. "He will live. I have made a fresh pot of coffee."

Gloria Johns volunteered to pour the coffee for everyone. She turned to Armand. "The same as usual, *chéri*?" she asked.

"*Merci, non*. I can pour my own coffee, like I can buy the groceries, drag them into the house and put them away. And then I can wash the dishes everyone has left everywhere and put them away too."

Michelle interceded. "Armand, you are being silly. You make it sound as if you are the only one who does anything around here. You have been like a bear with a sore head for the last three days, ever since we arrived."

"And why not? All everyone seems to want to do is play funny games, lie around and make jokes, all because there are no children. And then there is this business of the takeover. It is all very *stupide, non*?"

Michelle quickly came across to Armand and took him by the arm. "*Alors, c'est assez*. You are now behaving like a spoiled child."

"No, I am not behaving like a spoiled child, Michelle. First they play tricks on me, and then they spend their time talking about something which will not happen. A silly rumour and they become, how do you say, paranoid."

Brian Curtis spoke quietly from a large club chair in the corner by the landscape window. "It's not a rumour, Armand."

Armand crossed the room and sat down in the armchair opposite, his hands on his hips, looking for all the world like a pugnacious sumo wrestler. "And how do you know, Monsieur know-it-all D'Artagnan?" he asked sarcastically.

"Because this morning I phoned a friend who's a very senior executive at H & H. You and Michelle were out shopping when I phoned him on the spur of the moment. After a lot of arm twisting, he finally confirmed that the announcement of the takeover will be made when we return after the new year. Typically, it's meant to be very hush-hush. He wouldn't have told me anything if we hadn't been to college together, shared an apartment for two years, and remained very good friends ever since. He made me promise that I would say nothing to anyone before the announcement or he would be in all sorts of trouble. Only a handful of people at H & H and AgriBus know. Even our own divisional senior management don't know. It's all happened at the very top of both companies with the usual secrecy bull that goes on in these situations. Anyway, it looks as if the takeover is going to happen after all. And all of you have to promise not to say anything to anyone – no phone calls, no hints, nothing, especially after the announcement. This friend may very well lose his job if they find out he told me. When we return to work on Thursday next, you have to pretend you know nothing. I can't emphasize this enough, people. And that includes you, Ron. Nothing in your car repair shop, nothing to any customers. I don't have to remind any of you how quickly such a rumour will spread and someone is bound to ask where it started."

"I understand, Brian," Ron assured him. "Not a word."

"When I heard about the takeover being real, Armand, I had to tell the others and we decided we would go for a walk on the beach. We thought it would clear our minds so that we could work out how it might affect us. Which is why you came back to an empty house. In any event, let's all sit down and talk it through, if you like." Brian looked around for approval. "Let's sit around the dining room table. You too, Ron."

They arranged themselves around the table with their steaming hot cups of coffee.

It was Britt who broke the silence. "What I cannot understand is why AgriBus wants to sell us off in the first place. It is not as if the division is losing money, or we are not doing our jobs."

"At middle management levels, we'll probably never know the truth, but let's see if this makes sense," Brian volunteered. "There are a number of possibilities. It could be that H & H have made AgriBus an offer they can't refuse. They see things in the division which they need, either because we have expertise or products they want to exploit, or because there are marketing and distribution considerations which they can use to their advantage, maybe even both. Whatever the reason, their accounting and finance people think they can make money from the deal. Alternatively, AgriBus simply doesn't see the Ethicals Division as worthwhile continuing to bother with. It could also be that AgriBus can do better things with the money they can get by selling us off. In my opinion, it comes down to money every time, and how the accountants work the figures. Any other thoughts, anyone?"

Armand, who had listened attentively to Brian's explanation, snorted loudly. "Accountants! What do they know. They play with numbers and they forget about people. Before we came here ten years ago, I worked in a company that was taken over. Within three months, the new owners succeeded in destroying what had taken years to build: the way people work together and produce results. And then, when morale was low and productivity was down, they closed the place up, sold the land and buildings, put everybody out of work and made a huge profit. You know where they made the most money? From the employee retirement fund. Oh, yes, they offered us jobs at another factory, but on the other side of the city, two hours away in travelling.

Of course, if you did not accept their offer to work in the other factory and you had to resign, you lost all your benefits. That is how they got around the law and the agreement to protect the jobs and the retirement benefits of the employees. The whole affair was, how you say, shameful. That is what accountants do and that is what will happen to everyone in the division. Accountants do not care about people. All they can think about is money. Well, Michelle and I will not stay to see this happen. We return to France and we work the land and we make a living that way. Not so good, but we have control over our lives, *non?*"

There was silence around the table as they digested Armand's outburst. It was Gretl who asked the question which was on everyone's mind. "None of us are going to take you seriously about going back to France, Armand. But, just out of curiosity, how did the new owners destroy the morale of the workforce in such a short time, three months?"

"Very simple," Armand replied without hesitation. "First, they bribe the senior managers with the promise of a fat cheque if they behave themselves. What do you call that, Brian?"

"You're thinking of a golden parachute," Brian replied.

"*Absolument.* That is it. The senior managers have to agree to train the replacement senior management. They have to show these new managers where everything is: the accounts, the suppliers, the customers, the products, the people they must keep, the people they must fire, the good things, the bad things, everything. And they must also agree to leave everything behind when they leave the company. They must not take anything with them, and they must agree not to take jobs with the opposition, at least not for two or three years."

"How does that destroy morale, Armand?" Gretl persisted.

"Because then they begin to fire people, especially the older employees who have big salaries and big retirement benefits, and other employees who are not so good at their jobs. And as the first ones go, the rest begin to look over their shoulders and wonder who will be next. Maybe me, *non*? Maybe you? And so you stop working and you talk instead, you talk to other employees, you talk to other employers and, if you are very good, other employers talk to you. This is the best time to find good people. You are headhunted. But since most of us are so-so and we have little to offer that is important to another employer, we go into a corner and wait for the axe to fall. That is called 'low morale', *ma chère* Gretl, and it destroys the soul of a company. And I have seen it happen once and I never want to see it happen again. Which is why Michelle and I, we return to France as soon as we arrange our affairs. To go through something like this once in a lifetime is once too much."

"You know, Armand, takeovers don't *have* to be like this," Gloria Johns remarked thoughtfully. "When I was working many years ago, before Tony and I were married, my employer was made an offer he couldn't refuse. It was a small, privately owned company with less than a hundred employees, and he was a paternalistic and authoritarian old bastard. There were times when we hated his guts, but we knew that behind that gruff exterior, he did care about us. When one of us was in trouble, he was always there to help. But, most importantly, he made sure we understood what job security was all about. As long as we worked hard, and remained honest and loyal, we had a job. Sure, times were mostly good, but there were one or two very bad times also. You'll remember the early 1970s when things were very tough. Well, he never once put anyone off. But no one expected overtime and we had to watch every penny we spent. Hell, there were even weeks when we all wondered how he would meet the next wages bill, when there wasn't even enough left for him to pay himself. I know because I used to prepare the pay and keep the books on retirement and all the other little things he gave us when we made a heap of money, and which he never once suggested he throw back into the business to make things easier."

Gloria took a sip of her coffee and looked at the faces around the table. They were all clearly hanging on her every word. "Anyway, when he decided to accept the offer and run, he called us all into the warehouse. I remember it so well. He told us what he was going to do, and why. He explained that he was getting old, that he could no longer put the time and energy into the company to keep it viable. He told us that the company needed a heavy injection of money and technology in an increasingly competitive marketplace. It probably also needed younger and better-trained hands at the helm. It wasn't as if we didn't know all these things already. We'd been watching things get tougher all the time. Well, when he finished, there were tears everywhere, including his own. I have to admit, I was blowing hard in my handkerchief, and so were many of the men. But he made us a promise: he had agreed to sell out on very clear conditions, conditions which protected our jobs and the substantial benefits we had built up over the years. And the buyer stuck to the letter of that agreement."

Armand snorted. "No accountants, *hein*! So how did they do that?"

"On the first Monday after the deal was done, the new managing director brought us all into the warehouse and he told us that our jobs and our benefits were secure. He explained that, for the near future, it would be business as usual while they familiarized themselves with all the things that were going on. They did not propose changing anything until they understood exactly where the company stood. In the meantime, they had retained our boss for one year as a consultant and during that year they would make whatever changes were needed to bring us into the twenty-first century. He then went on to warn that some of us would have to adapt to new technology in the factory and the office. All attempts would be made to retrain us, but if some were not up to it, they would be let go with all their benefits and entitlements. And the new owners did just that for the next year. Then I met Tony, Andrew arrived soon after and I stopped working. I kept up with the news of the company for a while. All the things the new management had promised they would do, they delivered. It was all very professional and very well done. Let me add that it must have cost them a pretty penny to carry out that change programme, but they finished up with a workforce that was even more loyal and hardworking than we had been before the takeover. And that is worth a great deal. You know, the kinds of things people do or don't do, on the job and off the job, which make a company boom ahead – in other words, a high-morale company, Gretl."

Ron had been listening to Gloria with rapt attention. Now he surprised everyone by asking her, "What kinds of things?" Immediately, he was aware that he had suddenly become the centre of attention.

"An excellent question, Ronny," Britt reassured him. "Tell him, Gloria, please."

"I'm not sure I can do that very well, Ron, but I'll try. Let's say you're a worker in a factory and you walk past a machine and you see something wrong. What do you do? Well, you can either walk away from it because it's none of your business and you don't get paid to fix other people's problems, or you can report it to the supervisor. There is, though, a third possibility: you can approach the worker on that machine and you can tell him what you think is wrong. Now, he can tell you to go to hell, or he can thank you for pointing out a problem which will cost the company money if it isn't fixed as quickly as possible. In other words, it is everyone's responsibility to do whatever they can to prevent things from going wrong because it's like money out of your own pocket. And in every sense, it is. If there are enough of these problems which no one wants to fix before they begin to cost money, it begins to affect the bottom line. Alternatively, the less of these problems there are because everyone is pulling together, because everyone really cares what happens, the more successful a company is likely to be. And that can happen in the office as well, Ron. People sit and talk about problems, about better ways of doing things, of saving money. It can be as simple as switching off the light when you are last to go home at night, to coming back to work in the morning with a great idea that is going to improve something and therefore save money in getting the same job done, maybe even better than before. One last thing – it doesn't all happen just like that," she said, snapping her fingers. "It takes a lot to get people thinking like that, pulling together as a team. Well, enough of me. I think it's someone else's turn." Gloria sat back in her chair and looked squarely at Armand.

He smiled back at her and clapped his hands slowly. "In heaven, Gloria, these things happen. But not here on earth."

Michelle looked scathingly at her husband. "You are too cynical, Armand. Maybe it is time we went back to the farm, takeover or no takeover. If nothing else, a bit of physical work will make you lose some weight, instead of thinking that anything that's worth something can only happen in your head and can only be measured in dollars and cents."

Armand turned towards her, ready for a fight.

"Hey, you two, leave all that for the bedroom," Brian intervened. "I think Armand and Gloria have told us what can happen at the opposite ends of a continuum. And that was great, both of you. But is there a middle road, somewhere on earth, not in hell or in heaven?"

"I wasn't describing heaven, Brian," Gloria protested. "I was telling you what happened when a company wants to change a management style into what that company called a *high involvement workforce*."

"And I was not describing hell, thank you, Brian," added Armand. "I was describing what I saw with my own eyes. And *ma chère* Michelle knows exactly what I mean. I am not cynical, *madame*." He turned abruptly to his wife. "You were there with me. You saw how they played with the lives of people. You saw what became of a whole community. You saw the work of a whole lifetime disappear when the accountants took over. I was not exaggerating, Brian." Armand faced Brian once more. "These things happen, these tricks, these false promises, these lies. And I think you should all be ready when it happens."

"*If* it happens, Armand," Gloria pointed out.

"Oh, very well, Gloria. It is no use arguing. We can only wait and see." Armand stood and stretched. "I think it is time we all go for a walk, or have some lunch, or something. I am tired of this discussion that goes round and round."

Meanwhile, Ron and Britt had been talking quietly together. "Armand, Ron has something about these matters to say," Britt spoke out. "He also has had an interesting experience and I think we should hear him."

Armand looked across the table at Britt and Ron with an air of exaggerated tolerance. "Why not," he conceded, sitting down again. "I think we should all have something to say. We could have a round robin, *non*?"

"Only if we were playing ping-pong, Armand," Brian interjected, which broke up the tension as everyone laughed, including Armand. "OK, Ron, fire away."

"Well, this isn't about a takeover. But it is to do with trying to get everyone on side, just like Gloria was telling us. I was working for a tyre retreader some years ago – heavy, dirty, hot and smelly work, let me tell you. There were about twenty of us in the factory, including the factory manager who was always having to pitch in and help out on the machines. Anyway, things were always bad. The boss was lucky any day if he had fifteen out of twenty of us on the shop floor. And then there were men who received their pay on Thursday, pay day, you know, and we never saw them again. It was difficult finding people who wanted to work in that factory, so the boss used to wait outside the local jail on a Saturday morning, when men were let out, and he used to offer them a job, starting Monday first thing, with fifty dollars advance to see them through until their first payday. And a lot of the times he never saw them again, so he lost his fifty dollars, because, I mean, you know, it was no use advertising. Men came and had one look at the factory, saw the size of a bus or truck tyre, saw the lifting they would have to do and the working conditions, and you never saw them again. Let me tell you, it isn't a bit like the work all of you do at AgriBus – clean offices, labs, air-conditioning, computers, that sort of thing. I know you're all educated and the like, but this I'm telling you about was hard work and the pay was lousy."

"So, *mon ami*, what is it you are trying to say?" Armand asked impatiently. "Anyway, if it was so terrible, why did you work there?"

"As a matter of fact, I was there for almost two years. Why did I stay? Because I liked the work and I liked the men I worked with. I'd a lot of job satisfaction, if you know what I mean."

Armand leaned forward aggressively. "If I understood what you mean, I would not be asking."

Michelle bridled. "Armand, you are becoming impossible. If you do not want to listen, go for a walk. We want to hear what Ron has to say."

Britt also reacted to Armand's bad temper. "Armand, if I did not love you so much, my big French omelet, I would get up and hit you. You have given us more than enough trouble for one morning, thank you. Ron has never spoken about these things to me before and I want to hear him. And so do the others. Enough is enough."

Armand sat back in his chair, crossed his arms across his chest and raised his eyes to the ceiling. He was clearly bored with the whole conversation and the recital of personal experiences. He knew what he knew about takeovers, and that was that. It did no good talking about individual cases. Sure, there were always a few exceptional instances, but in the final analysis, it mostly came down to what the accountants worked out – what the fixed overheads were, how much return on investment could be expected, and what could be done to minimize one and maximize the other. Well, he would have to listen to this drivel whether he liked it or not, and it was too cold to go for a walk. Apart from which, he would certainly get a roasting from Michelle if he opened his mouth once more. But he had made it plain to everyone what *his* position was and he intended to stick to it, whatever funny little stories they told each other.

Gretl prompted Ron. "OK, Ron, back to you. We all want to hear what happened to you with that tyre retreader."

"All right, but if I didn't think it was interesting and relevant to your problem, I wouldn't open my mouth," said Ron. "Anyway, I worked there for about two years because I was nineteen, I enjoyed the heavy work which kept me fit, the job paid a bit more than I would make doing something else, and I liked making tyres. I know, that sounds a bit crazy, but it honestly gave me a great feeling inside to load a lousy-looking casing into a mould and twenty minutes later see a shiny retread come out. I also knew a lot of kids like me who used to buy these retreads and they were, well, kind of putting their lives in my hands. And the same went for the truckies and the bus drivers. These people trusted me to give them a tyre which would go the distance and would be safe. Anyway, we used to talk about these things in the lunch room, like what-did-it-all-mean type of thing. There was a small group of us, including the manager, who felt that way about our jobs – that it was important work we did. The new boys used to laugh at us for taking our jobs too seriously. But we did exactly that, take it seriously, I mean, which is why we stayed on when most of the others used to quit after a few weeks."

Ron looked at Britt, who was holding his calloused hand, and asked her. "How'm I doing, pet?"

"Just great, Ronny. Tell us more," and she gave his hand an especially hard squeeze.

"Well, about a year into the job we could see the boss getting pretty worried. His wife used to keep the books and do whatever needed to be done in the office. A good woman, like a big sister to all of us. Occasionally, she would make a joke about her husband when he was rushing in and out, or having to get stuck into a machine which had broken down, or whatever. And then she stopped saying anything, and we knew then that things were going bad. And one day, he brought this man into the factory and showed him what we did. And we thought he had come because he wanted to buy the place. White shirt, blue coat and tie, clean shoes. Anyway, the boss's wife tells us he's from the university and he wants to help her husband organize things differently so they can start making a bit of money."

Ron looked slowly around the table to make sure everyone was still interested. Even Armand had uncrossed his arms from his chest and was listening. "And the next week, the boss comes into the lunch room and sits with us and tells us he wants us to go with him to a resort in the mountains, a real nice place, where we can all sit together on a Saturday and Sunday, and talk. He's going to pay for everything, he tells us. All we need do is come and listen and, if we feel like it, we can say anything we want about the job and maybe even help him make a couple of decisions. He's going to pay us wages at normal time for the Saturday afternoon and all of Sunday. He calls this a business conference. So, the next Saturday, we all meet at midday at the factory and we load into a minibus – all, that is, except that new man, Ernie, who thinks it's a load of bull, and he has a new girlfriend and he knows who he'd prefer to spend his weekend with. And that guy from the university is with the boss and he introduces him as Dr John something or other, but to call him John. And then we took off. Well, some of the boys had brought their coolers with them, and they drank beer all the way up the mountain. And then, every so often, they'd yell for the driver to stop and they'd pile out and, you know, line up against the bus and wave to the cars that were passing by and hooting them. I could see the boss and Dr John look at each other when that happened, but they never said a word, all the way up. And then we were there, and it was a great place, with families and kids all eating in the same dining room with us and we knew this was going to be different and we had better stay sober and behave ourselves. And we did."

"So what happened at this business conference?" Tony asked, making a comment for the first time that morning. Everyone turned to him, feeling sympathy for him. For if there was one position which was vulnerable in the new takeover situation, it was Tony's. There clearly would not be room for another director of regulatory affairs in a combined operation, and H & H would almost certainly favour their own man.

Ron, however, was quick to react to Tony's question. "It was fantastic. After we had settled in, two of us sharing a separate cabin, and after dinner that Saturday night, we all went to a large room, which in fact was the loft of the dining hall converted into a meeting room. It had everything in it: a huge screen for watching films or videos, a very large table which had more than twenty chairs around it, then smaller tables in the corners of the room where half a dozen or so people could sit and talk as a work group, bookshelves against the back wall full of all sorts of management books and magazines and newspapers from all over the country, and some other countries as well, and a couple of cupboards full of everything you might want, you know, things like pens and flipcharts, that type of thing. Anyway, it was a great meeting room. First up, Dr John showed us a movie about two companies that had succeeded in changing their way of doing things and were making a heap of money. Very different companies, making very different things, and they each used different ways for making this change happen. I can even remember the word he used. It was *equifinality*. Big word, but all it means is, 'There are all sorts of ways of skinning a cat'. This Dr John was a really clever fellow. He would occasionally say something, but mostly he just asked questions and he got us talking so we were in there all the time."

Britt squeezed Ron's hand. "Ronny, what happened?"

Ron smiled at her. "I know. You want me to get to the end quickly. Well, you know, a lot happened that Saturday night and the next day. It changed my way of thinking completely, pet. None of us were the same after that. We began to think that maybe, just maybe, even working in a tyre-retreading factory could mean something worthwhile. I began to feel that I could get up every morning and honestly look forward to going back to work. And we did, most of us, after that weekend."

Brian Curtis' quiet voice cut through Ron's enthusiasm. "What caused the change, Ron?"

"Oh, many things but mostly it was the change in the way we were going to organize work and what Dr John called 'the reward system'. The film and the discussion on the Saturday night before we broke up got us all talking about how we might like to arrange the way we make decisions – for example, who decides how I do my work. That should be me, you know, since I'm the one closest to *my* job and, if I've been trained properly, I should do my job the way it fits me best, so long as it doesn't screw things up for other people. Most of us spent half the night talking about what we'd seen in the film and what it might mean for us. A couple of the men thought it was a whole bunch of bull but there were a few of us who were very interested in where all this was going to take us."

It was obvious that Ron was very keen to share his unique experience with the group. Brian had never seen his eyes shine so brightly, or his body language talk so eloquently. "So we were pretty primed up when we met after breakfast on Sunday morning. First of all, the boss got up and told us the money situation, warts and all. How much it cost to run the factory, how much profit there was in making a retread, how much money we could make out of the City Council bus tyres contract and what we were actually making, and so on. He told us what it cost to repair a machine, how many tyres each of us had to retread before we covered our wages, what it cost when one of us didn't turn up for work, what it cost to replace one of us when we quit, things like that. I tell you, I sat on the edge of my chair, and I could see all the others had their eyes wide open too. No one had ever told us things like that. Instead, it had always been, 'Get your head down and your tail up and never you mind what it all means. I know what's good for you and I know what's good for the company. Anyway, it's none of your friggin' business. I pay you to work, not to think.' That sort of thing. So we never cared about our jobs. To me, it was always how much I could get out of work. I used to play it for all it was worth, getting the most I could for the least possible work. Dr John called this attitude the *minimax principle*. I still do it, even though I now know there is a better way to get things done. But do you think I can get the bosses I've worked for to change their way of doing things? Not on your sweet life. They're all the same. Because they're bosses, they think they know everything, even the jobs we do on the shop floor. Well, let me tell you . . ."

"Ronny," Britt interrupted him, squeezing his hand very hard. "What else happened?"

"More importantly, Ron," Michelle cut in, "why did you leave your tyre company if things were that good?"

"Because what the boss said he would do, he didn't do. It didn't happen all of a sudden. It started OK. He said he would let us organize ourselves – who did what, when, how – that sort of thing, and that was fine. Within a couple of weeks after the conference we had sorted all that out and almost doubled our production because we wanted to make the new system work. On paper, we were making a heap of money. And we were trying to save it also. When a machine broke down, we didn't wait around until the boss or the factory manager had fixed it or the boss had brought in a repair man. We tried to fix it ourselves, and mostly we did. Most of the time, they were small things that we could fix ourselves. Anyway, that was fine."

"So what went wrong, Ron? The accountants took over?" Armand told Ron with a cynical grin on his round face.

"Actually, Armand, it *was* something like that. We had made an agreement on the mountain. We had made many agreements up there, but this was the most important one to us. If we made money, we had agreed we would share it, the employees and the boss. Every month, he was going to work out how much profit we had made, I mean, after he had paid all the bills. The net profit, I think it's called. Then he would pay himself a percentage on the capital he had invested in the business. We agreed on two percentage points above what banks lend you on a house. It was all a matter of risk, if you understand what I mean. What was left over, we would split in two, one-third going to him, two-thirds being split equally among all the employees, including his wife who was actually our bookkeeper and receptionist and was just another employee. Except that he owed so much to the bank that, by the time he had paid off the interest and some of the debt, there was very little left. Anyway, after six months when he brought us together and went through the accounts, what was left was still peanuts. He told us we had to pay off the debt to the bank and as soon as that was paid off, we would all be in the clear and the big payouts would begin. He didn't pay himself any profit share and he gave us what was left, which most of us really appreciated, even if it amounted to only a few dollars extra in our pay packets. But when we had almost finished paying off the bank, he made out that the business was worth a heap of money when all it was was a rented factory building, a bunch of old machines, most of them leased, a couple of old pick-up trucks and his almost new Range Rover, which was also leased by the company. So, after a further six months of all of us trying like hell, with weekly meetings to see what problems we had and how we should fix them, and monthly meetings where we were told how well we had done, there was still almost nothing in our pockets. First, a couple of the fellows stopped staying back to come to the meetings and hear the good news, if you know what I mean, and then they quit. And by the end of the year, things were almost back to what they had been before that weekend on the mountain. And then a friend of mine bought the service station where I'm at, and I went to work for him as a grease monkey, then doing simple repair jobs, and now there's not much on a car that I can't fix."

There was silence when Ron had finished. "What did Dr John say about all this?" Brian asked.

"Yeah, good question, Brian. To begin with, he would come to the weekly meetings and he taught us how to have an agenda, how to keep minutes in a special book, how to discuss things, how to problem-solve, points like that. And he also came to the first few monthly meetings and we could see he wasn't happy about the way the profit was being divided. And then he stopped coming and the boss said he'd stopped coming because he was very busy at the university. But we knew differently by then. We think he gave up on the boss because the boss was being too greedy. After all, money is like grease on an engine, it makes the wheels go round and it makes the engine work well. When there was so little grease going back into the engine, after a while the engine started creaking and groaning, if you know what I mean, and then it stopped going altogether. And that's when most of us quit trying, and then we quit working there altogether."

Michelle gave a big sigh and sat back in her chair. "*Quel dommage, n'est-ce pas?* What a pity, what a shame. It could have been so good for you. In your present job, Ron, you said you do not try very hard even though your boss is your friend. Why not? Have you told your boss about what you learnt at the tyre factory?"

Ron didn't hesitate. "Hey, Michelle, it seems like when it comes to money, no one is your friend. He gave me a job, sure, but he never said he wanted to share the profits with me. Yea, I told him about the tyre factory and what we did and why we tried hard. All he said to me was that running a business was never meant to be that way. People ought to be happy having a job. Anyway, why would he want to share the profits with me? Would I want to share the losses with him, that type of thing? So, now I do my job. I do it well because I like doing things well. It gives me job satisfaction, if you know what I mean. Anyway, if I screw up too often, I guess I wouldn't have a job. So, I do my job, and that's all."

Michelle sighed again. "Ron, that was fantastic, thank you. Don't you think so, Armand? Well, I suppose it is time for lunch, everyone, before Armand begins to argue with someone. What do you think, Brian and Gretl, it is your turn, *non*? I'm glad it is not the turn of Armand. The way he feels today, I think he would try to poison us all. So, we go for a little walk on the beach, or we go in the jacuzzi while you make the sandwiches."

Gretl and Brian stood. Brian gave Ron a slap on the back. "You did great. I haven't finished with you yet, young feller. I want to know a lot more. We'll talk after lunch, if that's OK with you," and he followed Gretl into the kitchen. But not without giving Armand, who had remained sitting in his chair with his arms crossed again, a huge wink. He called out from the kitchen. "Where did you put the arsenic, Armand? I thought I should put a heavy dose in your *jambon* sandwich, just to calm you down."

Armand called back. "It is not funny, D'Artagnan. I think you are all living in cuckoo-land. Anyway, we shall see what we shall see." And he rose, put his coat on and strode out through the back door onto the sundeck braving the elements. He had decided he would be as difficult as possible. And that was all there was to it!

After he had closed the door behind him, Michelle let out a little snigger, which was followed more loudly by the others who were getting up from the table. "I love him so dearly. But when he gets an idea in his head, that is the end of it, *non*? Anyway, you all know what he is like. He has to get out of these moods himself. I say we open a bottle of red wine, get in the jacuzzi and wait for lunch to come to us. Lunch is always something special when Gretl and Brian prepare it."

Chapter 3

10.30 p.m., Tuesday, 31 December

Tony Johns leaned over and kissed Gloria on the lips. He had obviously drunk too much, but she forgave him that. He was an amorous drunk, for which she had been eternally thankful. But she also knew he was very worried about his job now that he knew the takeover was a certainty. In any case, this was their last night at the beach house, Tuesday night and New Year's Eve, and they had just finished the most delectable dinner imaginable, accompanied by streamers, party hats, beautiful wines, the lot. They had started with fresh asparagus marinated in a special sauce which Michelle prepared in great secrecy and only when she had the kitchen to herself. This was followed by a small side dish of fresh grapes, strawberries and the most wonderful Brie, all soft and gooey, spread over thinly cut pieces of a very fresh and very crisp baguette. Armand had contributed this little aside, "to cleanse out the palate before the main course, you understand". And the main course, prepared by Gretl and Brian Curtis, had been superb. A whole filet mignon impregnated with fresh cloves of garlic, the filet rolled in olive oil and then covered with salt and black pepper. This had been accompanied by baked potatoes, pumpkin and lima beans, everything smothered in a thick béchamel sauce. And then a green salad sprinkled with feta cheese and black olives, prepared by Tony Johns, also to cleanse the palate. Finally, the *pièce de résistance*, the best apple strudel they had ever tasted, "just like my mother used to make" Britt reminded them a number of times as she became progressively more inebriated. This was covered with Gloria John's delightful homemade macadamia nut cream, the perfect complement for Britt's strudel.

And Ron had also truly excelled with a splendid selection of white and red wines to go with each of the courses, two bottles of French champagne to bring in the new year and, most amazingly, a couple of bottles of Galway Pipe Port which were almost impossible to obtain without a great deal of influence and/or coercion, neither of which they thought he possessed. But he had done his homework very carefully. He had studiously compiled, with considerable finesse, the full menu from everyone and, in collusion with a customer who was a wine buff, he had disappeared that morning and returned to the beach house with a large carton in his arms and a silly grin on his face. Britt had roundly rebuked him for drinking and driving, given him a big kiss and sent him to bed to sleep it off. They also noticed that, halfway through the afternoon, she also decided she would have a small rest and, when she finally reappeared, there was an even bigger grin on her face than Ron's. Clearly they had not had much sleep and had worked up an extraordinary appetite and thirst, which added considerable zest to the conversation during dinner.

"We have eaten too well," Armand declared, pushing his chair away from the table, straightening his yellow party hat and rubbing his big stomach. "Our last supper, do you think?" he added reflectively.

Michelle, who almost always reacted negatively to his innuendos when she had had too much to drink, turned sharply on him. "Armand, is this the way you keep your promise to keep your big mouth shut?"

Britt Berghoff quickly interrupted. She knew that look on Michelle's face too well. It spelt trouble, not just for Armand, but for everyone. She thought it would be good strategy to turn the conversation to something more serious than the provocative off-the-cuff remarks for which Armand was notorious. The subject she introduced had been on the periphery of her thoughts since speculation about the takeover had started. "Brian, how do you think they will make the announcement of the takeover?"

Brian was also anxious to deflect the mounting storm between the Herniers. He didn't wait for any further prompting. "The ideal way would be for the formal transfer of authority to take place before the whole of the division workforce. In other words, the chairman of AgriBus should gather everyone together, announce the takeover, any special conditions which might affect employees, and then hand over to the new chief who would tell us the whys and wherefores of the arrangement, no punches pulled, and lots of time for questions. Of course, it rarely happens that way. Sometimes, nothing is said and the rumour mill is allowed to run its full course, until major changes are suddenly introduced and heads begin to roll. But most times, the troops are fed a whole load of misleading nonsense. They're told it's business as usual, no one will be disadvantaged, the interests of everyone will be safeguarded, that kind of thing. What the new owners want more than anything is to ensure that no frustrated employee does something damaging: for example, erase all the customer accounts or the debtors ledger from the computer, walk off with some valuable piece of information and give it to the opposition, damage some important piece of equipment, and so forth. Also, the new owners will try and keep everyone in place and working, so that the business continues as before until they're ready to make the changes. What they don't want to see are key people being pirated away by other companies, which would have a negative impact on the performance of the new acquisition. In answer to your question, Beebee, I expect H & H will try and maintain the status quo in order to give themselves a chance to understand the business they have just bought before they start making changes."

"In other words, before they start firing people," Tony Johns interjected, a touch of bitterness creeping into his voice.

Gretl's reaction was surprisingly direct for her. "Oh, come on, Tony. This takeover is upsetting everyone and it's gone far enough. Maybe I'm being too sensitive, but ever since Brian rang Paul Ruffin at H & H . . ." She looked at her husband and rolled her eyes. "Sorry, dear, the name slipped out."

Brian Curtis pulled a wry face and shrugged. "It doesn't matter, sweetie. Maybe I've been too sensitive as well over this business. You were saying?" he prompted her.

"Well, ever since that phone call, there's been a shadow over everything we've done. I know jobs are often threatened when something like this happens, but it doesn't have to be like that, you know. Gloria told us about her experiences. Ron has described what can happen if the chief executive tackles problems constructively. And I'm sure there are lots of other examples where a takeover can mean all sorts of good things for everyone. I know there are horror stories out there, but why would H & H have to be one of these? In any case, I think we should wait and see what happens over the next few months. I can't imagine anything terrible happening to any of us. Hell, you're all highly skilled professionals, the kinds of people H & H would welcome in their organization. We've made a very real contribution to the ethical division over the years, especially you, Tony. You've often saved AgriBus's hide in their dealings with the government. I vote we try and see the good things that may come out of this takeover. It could mean all sorts of promotions, expanded opportunities, bigger challenges, bigger salaries, more perks . . . and lots more holidays together in this lovely old house. Enough of this talk of going back to France, Armand. You and Michelle are our dearest friends. We wouldn't know what to do without you. So, right now, on this our last night here, I want us all to put our hands together in the middle of the table, like we always do to celebrate our friendship on New Year's Eve, like good musketeers, and then I want to have some coffee, Ron, and a glass or two of your port in preparation for the new year. So, everyone, here's my hand in the middle of the table," and she pushed aside the plates to make room for the little ceremony and placed her hand on the table, palm down.

"Wow!" exclaimed Tony Johns. "If you make love like you make speeches, you're one hell of a woman, Gretl. Lucky fellow, Brian," as he quickly covered Gretl's hand with his own.

"And what's the matter with me, Tony Johns?" Gloria bridled. "Are you complaining about my performance, or are you being lecherous again?"

"Oho! I'm in the pooh, people," and he giggled drunkenly as he tried to give Gloria a kiss, missing her mouth and getting the side of her head, knocking her red and green party hat onto the floor in the process.

Brian had taken Gretl's other hand. "That was some scolding you gave us. And you're perfectly right. This business has been disturbing all of us. The first time we don't have the kids around our necks, the first time we leave them at home to fend for themselves and they appear to be doing splendidly, the first time we can properly relax for a week without a care in the world, and I had to make that silly phone call to Paul Ruffin at H & H. Incidentally, if I understand what is likely to happen, I wouldn't be surprised if Paul is the next CEO of the division. Whether that's good or bad for us, I have no idea. What I do know is that he's very ambitious, he wants to run his own show and has positioned himself at H & H to do just that – one foot in administration, one foot in the labs – although he's an animal pathologist like me. The reality is, folks, I don't know what's going to happen. Paul becoming the division manager is pure conjecture on my part. So let's not take this guessing business too far and, please everyone, not a word. I tell you, if this gets out, he'll nail my hide to the wall, especially if he becomes our new boss. And he would be perfectly justified, old friendships or not. Now, let's get on with the drinks and the coffee, and then let's all get in the jacuzzi and I expect everyone to go easy on the ogling of tits, bums and you know whats, especially you women. This is New Year's Eve and our last night here before we have to go back to work, as Gretl so forcefully reminded us. So let's forget about takeovers and have fun."

"Hear, hear," Britt added, "except that I want all you men to have a good look at my tits and my bum. When you get to my age, it is the thing I need most, men ogling me all over."

Ron, who had been busy in the kitchen getting coffee ready and opening a bottle of Galway Pipe, called out. "Don't you believe anything she says, you guys. We all know she's not backward in coming forward and you also know she's a real knockout. So keep your horny eyes off my old woman. Let me tell you, she's good for a lot of years yet. I may have to give her a new set of brakes, some new shock absorbers, maybe even a rebore, but she'll do me, if you know what I mean. Anyway, I think all you ladies are great and I think we men are all very lucky."

Britt called out to him. "Ronny, you'll do me too, and a little less about brakes and shock absorbers. I like the rebores, though. Now I'm going to go downstairs to the spa. Anyone who wants to see me do my dance of the seven veils can come with me. And, Ronny, you bring everything down there, especially both bottles of port and the champagne. Another fifty minutes to the new year and we still have some celebrating to do. And everybody, bring all the unfinished bottles of wine and your glasses. Waste not, want not, my mother used to say. Anyway, it's less to take home tomorrow."

Part II
Announcements

Chapter 4

7.00 a.m., Thursday, 2 January

Britt Berghoff leaned across the counter and retrieved Ron's empty plate. He leaned back in the swivel armchair and stretched with satisfaction. He had on clean blue overalls and heavy work boots and looked every inch the working man about to go on the job.

"You know, pet, I'm beginning to see why Germans are so fat. But what a way to go. You'll do me, for sure!"

"Ronny darling, you work hard all day and you usually do not have lunch, just maybe a sandwich and some coffee. If I do not feed you properly in the morning, how are you going to get your job done properly? The most important meal of the day is breakfast, you know that. Orange juice for vitamin C, cereal for your digestion, two eggs, sausage, bacon and toast to fill the empty spaces, and good strong coffee, and you are ready for a hard day's work. No?"

"Absolutely, pet. And since I get home well before you, I try to get some of the dinner ready. But I'll never be a cook like you. That schnitzel you prepared last night was something else.

And the kartoffel poofer – what can I say!" He blew her a kiss, which she returned with a big grin of satisfaction.

"Darling, it is such a pleasure cooking for you. You enjoy eating so much. Anyway, food means energy and, living with me, you need it. You know what they say about sex and Scorpios, and you are so good. Enough of that or I will take you back to bed, and then we will both be late for work. So, what is on the programme for you today? I think the garage will be full of broken cars, all of them belonging to young, beautiful women who are looking for boyfriends who are car mechanics. And here you are with a broken down middle-aged frau like me who should know better than to have such a young live-in lover."

"Oh, sure! Every morning, all these beauties line up and wait for me to pick which car I'm going to fix, depending on how available they are. Now listen, pet, I want to be serious for a moment. I wish I didn't have to come home with grease under my fingernails every night. You deserve better, being a top scientist and all, with your beautiful soft hands. I wish I was educated like you and you didn't have to put up with my calloused hands on your beautiful body. I also wish I knew as much as you, and I had travelled all over the world like you. I wish I enjoyed classical music like you, and I could read good books like you. Then we could talk about these things, and the concerts you take me to, and all them things. And I wish I could talk properly, like an educated man, and . . ."

Britt held up her hand and came around the bench. She took his young head between her gentle hands and kissed him on the mouth. "Enough now. You will learn all these things. I had to. I was not born with them already in my head, you know. And you are clever – as clever as me, maybe even better. It will come. But what is important is whether you enjoy your job. I know you pretend you like it, but you are frustrated. You want to go back to the tyre company, except you want to be able to run it like Dr John says it should be run, no?"

"Oh, you know that's just a pipe dream. Anyway, I don't want the retreading factory. I just want to maybe have a small company where we treat people right and they treat us right. I know it won't happen. I don't have the money to start my own business and, even if I did, I'd need a lot of help in bookkeeping, buying, dealing with the banks, all that sort of thing, to make it work. So, I'd better forget it and go on working for Joe."

"Not so fast, Ronny. What if you had enough money, and you had someone with you who knew about all these things you need to make your business go smoothly? Would you go ahead and do it? Here, have another cup of coffee. It does not matter if you are late today. You said this was important." Britt bundled her heavy dressing gown more tightly around her as she organized his coffee, poured one for herself, and came to sit on the other bar stool next to his. "So, speak."

"Well, I've been thinking. Every time we have a car come in the garage, there's almost always a need for a new part to replace one that's gone bad. Now, we carry a few things in the garage – hoses, spark plugs, fan belts, that kind of thing, parts that we know we'll need on a regular basis. But nine times out of ten we have to go to the office, find the right catalogue for the car we're fixing, turn to the model, the year, then find the right part number, tell them in the office what part we need, then they phone a spare parts place, and so on. Maybe an hour later, if we're lucky, we get the part by special courier. Sometimes we've other work to do on other cars, but most times we pretend we have something else to do on the same car until the part arrives. And we charge the customer for most of that downtime and we absorb the rest, which is money lost for everyone."

"So?" Britt prompted him.

"Well, what I thought we should have is something between the parts warehouse and the repair shops, something on wheels with an inventory where we have most of the parts you might need, with a phone and a small computer which tells you if a part is on board, and how many, and the quickest route to get to the customer. All these things already exist but in different computer programs. I've done my research in the computer magazines I get each month. It's all there except I don't think anyone has put the bits and pieces together in a complete software package yet, so that we can provide quick service to the repair yards at a much better price."

"So, you are talking about putting a parts warehouse on wheels, in large vans with a good inventory on board, each van having a territory, each van driver trained to work a specially programmed computer and to deliver the parts quickly to the repair shops. Very interesting, Ronny. And you would be in charge to make sure the vans were in good working order, all the parts were on board each day, and the van drivers knew how to use the computers well. And you would then do what Dr John said should be done in your business: lots of helping each other to keep the customers happy, lots of saving and making money, and some profit sharing, maybe everyone even having some shares in the business so they feel it is their business, not just a place where they work, that sort of thing."

"You got it, pet. I could do the outside work, but there would have to be someone inside who looked after things – buying, payroll, making sure everything was going smoothly so the people on the front end had the support they needed. You need an organization, and lots of money, and I've got neither. So it's all a pipe dream, like I said, and I'll still be getting grease under my fingernails, working for someone else, till I die. And now I'd better get going, pet, before Joe gets mad and fires me, and then I won't even have that job." He pulled Britt off the chair, gave her a big kiss, and went on his way. She followed him to the door of her house and waved as his small, red roadster disappeared down the drive in a squeal of tyres and a small cloud of exhaust fumes.

Britt thoughtfully returned to her chair and her unfinished coffee. It sounded as if Ron had a good idea. Certainly, it would need money to get the project going, but, she knew that that was never the main problem. What was far more important in starting a business was the potential of that business, and the people behind it. She couldn't help smiling to herself. She had never told Ron what she had done for the first ten years of her working life, before she had decided to become a scientist. It was certainly an odd coincidence that she should have been heavily involved in a business which was not unlike Ron's idea, except that it had been in a wholesale pharmaceutical company, delivering everything, from bandages to blood to bromides, to medical practices and small hospitals on a needs basis, just like the car repair business.

Her breakfast talk with Ron had provided an interesting few minutes of soul baring. She would tuck these revelations about her much-loved Ronny away in the back of her mind. She had decided, years ago, never to predict the future. After all, who would have said she would one day leave a very well-paid job as the office manager of a highly efficient and profitable wholesale pharmaceutical company, to go to university and complete a doctorate in toxicology with first-class honours. Who would have predicted she would then go to work for AgriBus, becoming the senior toxicologist of their Human Ethicals Division within five years. But then, who would have thought she would fall head over heels in love with a much younger man who had never completed the tenth grade.

It was time to get ready for work. Britt rose from her chair, busied herself tidying the kitchen and went into their bedroom. She threw her dressing gown on the bed and stopped for a moment nude in front of the full length mirror. She looked pretty good for an ageing scientist, she decided, and sashayed sensuously past the mirror into the bathroom.

Gloria Johns took the four plates of steaming porridge from the kitchen workbench to the breakfast table and headed for the stairs leading to the mezzanine bedrooms. "Come on everyone. The porridge is on the table and I don't want it to get cold," she called out. She waited for a response. There was complete silence. "Tony, Samantha, Andrew. Did you hear me?"

Tony Johns appeared at the top of the stairs in his navy blue pinstripe suit, white business shirt, club tie, briefcase in hand, the perfect bureaucrat on his way to work. He came down the stairs one slow step at a time.

"Dragging your feet a little, darling?" she asked him, raising an eyebrow quizzically. "I don't suppose it has anything to do with returning to work after our week at the sea, or the bender you had on New Year's Eve, or the two too many drinks you had last night?" She waited for a reply, but he edged past her with that sheepish grin she had come to recognize so well as a sign of guilt or uncertainty. She had never quite worked out which over their twenty-one years of marriage. She thought it might be the latter this morning, his thoughts firmly fixed on the forthcoming takeover. "One step at a time, Tony dear. You can't let this takeover business upset you, certainly not until the announcement is made, and not much even then. You must wait till someone talks to you about taking early retirement, if someone talks to you at all. And even then you won't be sure. In the meantime, let me tell you, your face is like an open book for those of us who know you well. And that means half the employees of the division. Don't forget what Brian asked us all to do, which was what?"

"I know. Not to show, by any means, that we know the division is going to H & H. I promise I'll be completely inscrutable once I get to work. But I can't help feeling this year is going to be different somehow. Don't ask me how I know, but I do." He gave her another of his sheepish smiles, and sat in his customary chair at the head of the table, the morning sunlight pouring through the French windows leading out onto the sundeck. "I suppose I'd better get your porridge into me and take off. Wouldn't you know," he continued, turning around to look at Gloria's well-ordered garden through the window, "the weather has to be great just when you have to go back to work." He looked quickly at the electric clock on the wall above the sink. "I'd better get on with it. Wouldn't do to be late for my own funeral."

Gloria threw her hands up in exasperation and took her place opposite him at the table. "Tony, you are, without a doubt, the most depressing and the greatest 'self-fulfilling-prophecy' person imaginable. Leave it alone. If you lose your job, there'll be other jobs that will be just as good, maybe even better. Anyway, you've been at AgriBus too long. You were complaining before we went away that you were getting stale. I want you to think for a moment of the worst that can happen. The children are almost off our hands. Andrew has one more year at college and Samantha finishes high school at the end of the year. She wants to find a job and a place of her own for the next year or two. And we have some savings. We're a lot better off than most. Look at the Walsh's. Now, there's a family who're having a hard time making ends meet with their four problem children, even with Martha working part-time. We have two healthy, well-adjusted children, we have a good roof over our heads, and we have each other. We have so much to be thankful for, but you insist on seeing shadows in all the dark places, instead of the sun pouring through the windows. Now finish your breakfast and go to work and let tomorrow look after itself." She spooned some porridge into her mouth. "Ugh! It's tepid. All your fault, Tony Johns. And where are these children of ours?" She stood and went to the foot of the stairs, calling for them to come to breakfast this instant.

Tony Johns watched her move purposefully across the kitchen and up the stairs, his face twisted in the most sheepish grin he could muster. How could he explain to her that his fears were not related to how much money they had, or how lucky they were to all be healthy and surrounded by good friends. What it had to do with was the very real possibility that, at his age, he might never find another job. He was almost fifty-three. He could remember so clearly when he had been out of work for almost six months many years before, soon after they were married. It hadn't been the money then, although they had had to do without a great deal. It had to do with the inactivity which joblessness brought with it. It had to do with getting up in the morning and saying to himself, "What do I do today? Maybe there's a job going in the Tuesday, or is today Thursday, newspaper?" although he knew most jobs were advertised on Saturday. He so often lost track of the days. They seemed to run into each other in a never-ending routine of purposeless make-do activities. And then he knew the statistics: 85 per cent of these jobs had already been filled, but they had to be advertised to satisfy some arcane desire by senior management to see what was out there, or to play fair with the public at large by letting them know a job had become available . . . even if it already had someone firmly in it! And then the next 10 per cent would be filled through the old boy network. Which left 5 per cent of advertised jobs that were genuinely available, with everyone and his dog after them. It had been a soul-destroying period in his life and he didn't want to go through it again. At his age, he was not ready to retire from an active working existence which continually stretched him intellectually and kept him alive, however much he complained. Yes, alive! During that jobless period, he had felt so often as if he were slowly dying. And now, when the job market was so much tougher, he would have to get out once again and forage about, that awful feeling of hopelessness slowly growing until you stopped sending off the applications, and then you even stopped reading the advertisements. If only Gloria fully understood what he thought he might have to go through, she would be a lot more sympathetic. No, not sympathetic, he reflected. He didn't want her sympathy. He just wanted her to be a little less critical.

Well, he had better get on with it. He had a great deal to do. The government inspectors would probably be waiting for him in the lobby, hoping to find some fault in the production system, some piece of paper out of place, some routine not being carried out to the letter. And he would have to explain, then cajole, even coerce, eventually arrange to have the company technocrats meet with the government bureaucrats to show them why they had deviated from a minor set procedure. And so it went on, seemingly boring, but very important work. He was the man who threw the calming oil on the troubled waters of government regulations intended supposedly to protect the public from itself.

He rose from his now empty plate just as Gloria returned, shepherding their two recalcitrant grown-up children to the table, complaining they didn't have to get up so early, just because Dad had to go to work. Anyway, they hated porridge.

He decided he would escape from all that. Let Gloria deal with these fractious moments of family dissent. He would go and do battle with the world, tackling the problems that appeared at every bureaucratic turn in the corporate road. He gave her a quick peck on the cheek and waved vaguely in the direction of his offspring. Then he headed for the back door and his wonderfully reliable Toyota estate waiting for him in the drive as it had done for almost eight years without once letting him down. He had been lucky with that car. It had clearly been assembled on a Wednesday. These days, however, he had begun to expect that a main component would wear out soon and his children would urge him not to spend any money to have it fixed, to get rid of that piece of junk, get something new, something flashy, something they could borrow to impress their friends. That seemed to be the essence of life in this increasingly materialistic age – all speed, show and glitter. And in the middle of this fast lane were an eight-year-old car and a fifty-three-year-old corporate lawyer, both ready for the scrapheap, but desperately trying to keep up.

He turned the ignition and the engine immediately sprang to life. Like his car, he was not yet ready for the scrapheap. He would show them. And if he had to, he would surprise them all and go down fighting. He let go the handbrake and the car bounded down the drive, onto the road, past a Range Rover as if it were standing still, fast round the next corner, tyres screaming. He entered the main traffic with a kick of his heels and a roar at the much newer models. "Out of my way, you amateurs, I'm coming through."

Armand Hernier cherished these moments most of all. A large cup of black coffee, sitting at the breakfast table in his silk pyjamas, satin dressing gown and lambswool slippers, reading the paper and, most importantly, alone. What he had increasingly come to hate was the brashness of youth. Most mornings he had to salvage what was left of the paper after Guy and Honorie had gone through their favourite sections and left it in complete disarray, quite often in different parts of the house. Well, he had the house all to himself, the paper had not been touched, and he could luxuriate for the first time since they had returned from their week at the beach.

Guy and Honorie, the retards, as he sometimes liked to call the two children still left at home, had disappeared very early and, he expected, were meeting like-thinking retards in some overpopulated and unsavoury apartments somewhere downtown. He had no wish to know, nor did he want to continue to urge them interminably to take life much more seriously. But then, why should they. *Grandpère* Lucien had left each of his three grandchildren a sizeable chunk of money which they would inherit at the age of twenty-five. As far as these two younger of his three children were concerned, they had some time ago realized they had little to worry about for some considerable proportion of their lives, even if they were entirely profligate. If only *grandpère* Lucien had realized what his generosity would produce. Like any good Frenchman who had garnered a considerable fortune by dint of hard work and frugal living, he would very quickly have changed the terms of his will and forced these two young people to reassess the wisdom of their ways. But *grandpère* Lucien had timed his death too well, and now his son-in-law, Armand, was faced with this ridiculous problem. However, thank heaven for his eldest son, Maurice, the apple of his eye, who was currently completing a doctorate in inorganic chemistry and wanted nothing better than to find a cure for AIDS, heart disease, even old age.

He often wondered at the unpredictability of life and the outcomes of decisions. He remembered so well *grandpère* Lucien's dictum, "Decide in haste, repent at leisure", which was precisely what he was doing at the moment, on a whole manner of issues. He and Michelle had wanted three children, but they had not bargained on only one out of three deciding to take life seriously. The younger two expected their mother to do everything for them, and expected their father to allow them to live at home indefinitely for nothing and to drive an expensive sports car each, which they had purchased by borrowing, at outrageous interest rates, on their anticipated inheritance. It seemed to Armand he would never see them do anything of value. They never had so far and, he was pessimistic enough to believe, they never would. So much for his less than illustrious two younger offspring. And, with the best will in the world, there was nothing he could do about it, not so long as Michelle threw her mother's mantle of forbearance over them and forgave their every transgression as mere peccadilloes attributable to their youth. They would grow up one day, she constantly reassured him, let him but wait and see; they would surprise him with their achievements, and he would have to admit, especially to them, how terribly wrong he had been.

As for Michelle this morning, she had left early for her part-time job in the local pharmacy where, for three days a week, she was an occasional salesperson. The job filled in part of her week and gave her pocket money – which she hardly needed given *grandpère*'s munificence – thus enabling her to play tennis twice a week and then go on after tennis to her bridge club. She adored both pastimes, and she maintained, they kept her sane. He had always resented her these pleasures, having tried unsuccessfully to join her in both, but finding she was so much better at them than he. Somehow his body let him down at tennis, a not altogether surprising result given his weight and physical condition, and his mind had never managed to discipline itself sufficiently for him to be a good bridge player. Not that he hadn't tried other hobbies over the years – swimming, archery, backgammon – but he had found them all somewhat boring and had eventually abandoned them. He had even tried his hand at golf, which had turned out to be the single most frustrating experience he had ever endured.

What he did have, however, was a mind which would have

impressed de Bono and which made him such a fine research chemist, seeing fresh connections in the most unlikely places and generating some exciting initiatives. Well, certainly he had plenty of ideas, but the follow through in AgriBus was terrible. It took forever to get anything approved for development. He knew development was expensive, but why be in pure research, he often asked himself, if you couldn't afford it, or you didn't want to make the investment. Which is why he admired Brian Curtis so much. Without Brian's plodding support in Development, they would have been making generic drugs to be sold over the counter in supermarkets instead of looking for the big breakthrough which would make reputations and a billion dollars.

He sighed as only he could sigh, Michelle maintained, a long, doleful breathing in, and an equally long, doleful breathing out. It brought tears to the eyes, it was so sad. Well, maybe H & H would give him a little more freedom to practise his profession. It couldn't be worse than at AgriBus. He sighed again and set the paper aside. Here he was, in the singular situation of being perfectly alone, no one to disturb him or separate him from his beloved newspaper, and all he could do was sigh, think about the frustrations his work brought, and wish selfishly that the takeover would give him greater research opportunities, without a thought for the consequences the takeover would have for other less fortunate employees – the scientists and technicians in Development, and the people in Sales and Marketing. He would have to wait and see what happened, but he knew, deep down, that there would be blood all over the floor. There had to be. It was inconceivable that some heads wouldn't be required to move and others to roll. If he were in charge, a whole range of economies would be immediately instituted. It was impossible to ignore them, not when you combined two organizations with similar interests and technologies, and one the size of H & H. Tony Johns was a certainty to go. Maybe Britt Berghoff. Even Brian Curtis might be in danger of being made redundant. The fact that he himself was in pure research insulated him somewhat from redundancy. If H & H wanted anything most of all, it would be the pure research aspect, and they would therefore need people like him, even if it meant that he might have to move to another location to keep his job. He sighed again. It would be a difficult period ahead and he hated the idea of having to console friends who would be let go by the merged company.

He turned once again to the newspaper, but his thoughts were elsewhere. Having read the headline of an article three times without understanding it, he decided he would not be able to read his newspaper after all, in spite of the ideal conditions that existed for this activity. He put the paper aside, refilled his cup of coffee from the electric coffee pot which was always on, added his two spoons of sugar, and wandered across to the window overlooking the park across the road. He would need to get ready for work very shortly.

He had always liked going to work – occupying his comfortable office, walking around his laboratory, discussing work in progress with his colleagues, examining the status of his various research projects – all very absorbing and highly satisfying. But this morning, he wasn't looking forward to it one little bit. Somehow, he knew the situation would be different. What made it worse was that he would have to pretend he knew nothing about the takeover, which would be difficult for him to do, unlike his other fellow musketeers, it seemed. And how long would he have to go around ignoring the rumours which were bound to circulate, maybe even denying that he knew anything about a takeover? It was not in his nature to dissemble, and this would be hard for him to carry off. And what if one of the other musketeers cracked and revealed they had known about the takeover all along? What would he say to his colleagues in the research division? How could he explain to them that Brian Curtis had bound him to secrecy because he didn't want to embarrass his future H & H boss? How would his silence and seeming insincerity appear against the likelihood that a number of them would be out of a job – in some cases, sooner rather than later – with little or no chance to look around, pull in favours, network madly, explore possible openings, and all the other positive steps one should take before the axe came down? This was ridiculous. How could he have allowed himself to be placed in such a position, he, Armand Hernier, who always spoke his mind about anything and everything, who was always open, maybe even to a fault.

Armand drank the remainder of his coffee in quiet desperation. One thing he knew. He could not let Brian Curtis down, however uncomfortable the next few days might become. He would have to put up a pretence, deny he knew anything about the takeover, maybe even lie, until the announcement. All he could hope was that that announcement would be made as soon as possible and cut short his agony. Well, that was that. He turned away from the view of the park, the window, the newspaper lying unread on the breakfast table, squared his shoulders and marched with determination to the bedroom. If nothing else, he would face the world with true Gallic courage and fortitude.

Brian Curtis looked around the corner of his half-open office door. Nancy Barnett and Holly Notts were deep in conversation by the window. He had not expected either of these two women to be in so early on this first business day of the year, and certainly not in his office, obviously waiting for him to arrive. Nancy, the secretary he had shared for a number of years with the other senior scientists in Pathology, and Holly, a junior technician in their department who had started with them about halfway through the previous year, did not see him as he came slowly through the door.

"... but I would be first to go. Last in, first out, and I don't have formal qualifications, just hands-on experience. I love my job and I love the experimental animals. Anyway, I need my job badly now that Mark's business has folded. We could lose our house, everything, if I was fired from AgriBus." Holly took hold of Nancy's arm, her voice shaking at the likelihood of such an event occurring.

Nancy put her arm around Holly's trembling shoulders and gave her a hug, trying to comfort her. "I don't know where your bank contact got that information, Holly, but I'm sure he's completely wrong. There's no confirmed takeover of HED that any of us has heard of. Wild rumours, yes, but this is just crazy talk. Look, sit down. As soon as Dr Curtis comes in he'll tell you and that'll be the end of the story, OK?"

Brian pushed the door open further and walked in, dropping his briefcase on the floor by his desk. "Good morning, ladies. And a happy new year to you both. This is a pleasant surprise. I hardly expected to see either of you much before nine o'clock. Anyway, what am I supposed to tell you, Holly, which brought you in so early on this sunny morning?" Brian stepped to the window and waited, every nerve fibre in his body awake to the possibility he would have to pretend he knew nothing about the takeover. He might even have to lie brazenly to people he had respected and liked for years, in particular Nancy Barnett, as loyal and hardworking a secretary as anyone would ever want.

"My apologies, Brian, but Holly's been told the division has been sold to H & H. She heard it from the deputy manager of her bank. He's in charge of loans, that type of thing. He rang her the other day to ask if there was any possibility she might lose her job. He wanted to make sure she understood he was concerned about their house loan since Mark had closed his furniture-repair business in the fall and was struggling to find the money to pay off his creditors. If she were also to lose her job . . . well, he said to her, he would have trouble letting them hang on to their new home, that sort of thing. She's been worrying about this right through the Christmas break and thought she would come in early and try to find out if there was going to be a takeover and, if so, was she likely to lose her job."

Brian Curtis pushed himself away from the window and sat in his desk chair. He gestured vaguely at the chairs on the other side of his desk. "Let's all sit down and take it easy," he told the two women. He waited until they were settled. "I don't have to tell either of you of the rumours that are forever going around any organization. AgriBus is no exception. The question you want me to answer is whether I know something everyone else doesn't. In other words, is HED the subject of a takeover, and, more specifically, is it being acquired by H & H? Like yourselves, I've heard talk that this is in the wind. I can't tell you any more than that. But even if HED is taken over, what happens to your job, Holly, or your job, Nancy, or mine, for that matter? I have no idea on that score, but I would like to think that all of us in HED are gainfully employed. We have very real jobs to do and, unless our jobs can be done elsewhere by other people, there's no reason why we should be asked to go. In other words, we all appear to have secure jobs. However, given your particular circumstances, Holly, should you cover yourself by looking for another job in another more stable company? I can't answer that. At this point, there has been no official announcement about a takeover. I can only tell you that various people have heard something from someone, like you have from your bank man, so we all have to take the matter a little seriously. If it's true and HED is going to H & H, then we go with it. Will new management fire us? I can't imagine why. It may happen. If it does, I expect we shall be given some notice, weeks, if not months. We won't be asked to go overnight, I'm sure." He waited for his words to take effect.

The two women looked at each other. Holly Notts spoke out first. "I've been under a lot of strain about Mark's business, about our debts, you know, money things, Dr Curtis. And when Mr Rush, the loans manager, phoned to ask how secure my job was, now that HED was being taken over, I didn't know what to do. I stewed about it over the Christmas holiday, and I decided I needed to talk to someone who could tell me. I thought I should ask Nancy, but she was away. I didn't want to speak to anyone else. We all trust her, if you know what I mean. Which is why I phoned her at home last night and she told me to come in early because you always come in early and I could talk to you, and if anyone knew about the takeover, it would have to be you. I feel a lot better now, Dr Curtis. I'm sorry I bothered you. At least I know if I get fired, it won't be because you don't need me anymore. It will be because someone else wants to get rid of people like me. I also understand we will all be given some time to find other jobs and, let me tell you, I can turn my hand to anything, including looking after lab animals like I'm doing now. So, I won't keep you any longer. Thank you, Dr Curtis, and thank you, Nancy. I do appreciate your help." Holly Notts rose hurriedly and quickly left Brian's office, closing the door behind her.

Neither Brian nor Nancy said a word for a while. Nancy rose from her chair and went to the window. "I've never heard such bullshit from you before, Brian," she informed him without turning her head away from the scenery. "Something's going on, isn't it? These dickheads in the boardroom have sold us down the river, haven't they? And don't try pulling the wool over my eyes, Brian Curtis. I know you too well. So, let's have the truth."

Brian couldn't help smiling. Nancy had been with Pathology for over seven years and, during that time, she had come to know him almost as well as Gretl, maybe even better. Secretaries were like this. It was always a matter of being two steps ahead, better still, three steps ahead of their bosses. And she was that, and more. And she knew when he was spinning someone a line, and when he was being genuine. She had just seen him spin Holly Notts a very good line, and she didn't like it one bit. And he knew she knew he had been procrastinating as never before. She was expecting an answer from him, and he knew she would know immediately if he tried to fob her off. So, what to do? One thing he could not do is tell her that Holly Notts' bank man was right. Where that man had received his information, he would probably never know. What he could do was tell Nancy that he couldn't confirm it, one way or the other – and she would then know that the Human Ethicals Division was going to Helm & Hathaway. And she would want to know how he knew for certain. And he would have to tell her he couldn't tell her. And not to tell one's secretary about an important company matter was almost as serious as not telling one's priest in the confessional about a grievous sin one had just committed.

He gave her a wry grin and a shrug as she looked down at him from her position by the window, waiting impatiently for his reply. She didn't hesitate. She nodded her head and stormed out of his office leaving the door ajar. He had just severely damaged a very close relationship, one that had taken years to build and had stood the test of time. But what else could he do, he asked himself? He only hoped that saying nothing about his source of information, about Paul Ruffin at H & H, would be guarded as jealously by the other musketeers. Because, if one of them didn't, well . . . too late to think about the consequences now.

Chapter 5

4.00 p.m., Thursday, 2 January

Brian stood at his office window and looked over the scene of activity below. He was joined at the window by Britt and Armand. The three stood quietly watching workmen erecting a huge marquee on the immaculate lawn bordered by the circular drive at the front of their building.

"It is a very large marquee, Brian," Britt observed.

"They expect everyone in the division to attend," Armand commented. "And why not, *mes amis*, the rumours are flying around like confetti in a strong wind. The notice of the meeting has gone up on the notice board downstairs. Tomorrow, Friday, at 4.00 p.m., about the time all the workers leave for the weekend. They do not want to waste any company time, they think. As if anyone is going to do any work from now on anyway. Sometimes I think senior administrators are the stupidest people in the world. Well, it will be an interesting meeting, *non?*" Armand threw his large bulk into the nearest chair and emitted one of his doleful sighs.

Britt raised her arms as if warding off some physical threat.

"If you throw yourself onto the furniture like this, there will be little left for H & H to take over, my ripe piece of Roquefort."

"Enough with the jokes, Beebee. I am not in the mood," Armand replied, his forehead creasing in frustration. "There are a lot of worried people out there. They are asking if H & H will shut the place down, if they are going to have jobs this time next week, if they are going to have to move their families to some other place, if they are . . ."

Britt interrupted him and leaned over to give him a peck on the forehead. "Forgive me, Armand. Sometimes I behave like an idiot, but you know I would not hurt your feelings for anything in the world, not intentionally."

He waved his hand in acknowledgement. "I know, *ma chère* Beebee. It is just that I do not like to see things like this happening to people who depend so much on their jobs . . ." He paused in mid-sentence. "It is my turn to apologize, my very good friends. You have heard this sermon from me before, *non*?" He stood, gave Britt a quick kiss on the cheek, slapped Brian on the shoulder and went out, closing the door behind him.

Britt and Brian continued to stand at the window as the marquee began to take shape. Trucks were pulling up and depositing mountains of chairs, platforms, electronic equipment, loudspeakers, everything either of them could imagine would be needed for a mass meeting.

"Our beautiful lawn will not be the same by the time they finish."

"I was thinking the same thing, Beebee. Let's hope it doesn't rain between now and four tomorrow afternoon or our beautiful lawn will be the biggest mud patch you can imagine."

Britt continued watching the activity below for a few moments longer and nudged Brian in the side. "I suppose I had better go and do some work. I'll see you later, darling."

Brian sat at his desk and tried to focus on a report which lay half-read in front of him, but he couldn't. He set it aside, switched his computer to "Games" and thought he would play a few hands of solitaire. He almost invariably found playing a card game of some kind relaxed him and he was able to return to his work with a strangely refreshed mind. Not this time! By the third game, he decided he would have to do something else. Perhaps the answer was for him to take a walk around the animal laboratory. Watching the lab mice in their various cages had also had a calming effect on him in the past. Anyway, he might just find someone interesting to talk to, except that he expected the conversation would centre on the announcement on the notice boards and the memo all supervisory staff and above had received soon after lunch. He had spent more than enough time talking over the matter during the past week and he hoped he might share some different fare. After all, all the employees of HED had just come back from a week away and many would have had an interesting time, if only because they had gone to spend that period with family or friends elsewhere.

He walked down the passage, past half-shut office doors with their occupants seemingly immersed in their work, past open office areas where technicians had their heads buried in computers, or were busy writing, or speaking on the phone in hushed voices. Where he had expected to find small groups around the coffee machines talking about the meeting, what he found were people who were keeping their heads well down and out of sight, determined to exhibit work habits on this first day of the year which would not compromise them in any way. It was not what he or Armand or Britt had thought would happen, and yet he was also conscious that the other two had not spent much time away from their jobs. An interesting and unexpected reaction, given that everyone in the division would have a good idea what the meeting was about by now. All that was missing were the details and they would have to wait till the meeting for those.

Brian decided to return to his office and do what everyone else was doing. He would leave his door half-open so that anyone passing by would see him hard at work.

Chapter 6

7.00 a.m., Friday, 3 January

Brian Curtis backed into his car space. It made him feel guilty having a reserved car space near to the building. He had argued consistently that just because he was one of the twenty or so most senior managers in HED didn't entitle him to that particular privilege. Pregnant women and older people should have the car spaces closest to the building. However, at the infrequent and irregular management meetings when he had raised the issue, he had been shouted down by his colleagues who, almost unanimously, felt they deserved that perk not only by right of organizational seniority, but, more importantly, by need. After all, they pointed out, they had put in their time in universities, then in the business world, and now in long hours at work and high-stress jobs. In addition, it made economic sense that, since all of them were paid big salaries, they should be able to get to their desks as quickly as possible and not have to take up valuable company time fighting for a car space with some petty clerk in some remote corner of the car park. Which is why he always backed into his car space. He considered that a type of penance for having been singled out by some omnipotent power for favoured treatment over most of his fellow workers.

He got out of his car, sniffed the air and, on the spur of the moment, decided he would walk around the building and see what had been accomplished on the front lawn. He hesitated for a moment as he went past the back door, his special pass key in the hand. Why did he suddenly feel guilty for wanting to have a look? If someone saw him, would they think he was some sort of Peeping Tom? After all, he would see it soon enough, at four o'clock that afternoon, with another four hundred or so people. Nonetheless, the size of the marquee looked impressive from his third floor office window. It would seem even more impressive from the inside, especially if it was empty of people. He would have a look, and hang the consequences!

There was a well-laid-out concrete path around the building and, as he rounded the corner, he came in sight of the marquee. He stopped and looked over that immense dark green canvas structure. It blotted out the sky. He had never seen anything like this except at the circus, on the rare occasions when he had been indulged as a child, and then once more when Kimmy was three or four. He crossed the circular drive and walked in. The lawn had been covered by a special outdoor green carpet which had obviously been made to fit between and around the two dozen or so huge wooden supports which held the marquee up. The chairs had been arranged in a semi-circle around a long platform about three feet off the ground, allowing the audience an uninterrupted view of the people sitting on the platform and speaking at the lectern. On either side of the lectern were two huge video screens, and immediately above and behind it, a large screen, almost as large as those found in cinemas. Positioned strategically around the marquee were large black loudspeakers, fed by a network of power and communication cables hanging from the supports, which ran in every direction, and especially towards the platform, with its huge screens.

He marvelled at people's ingenuity. In a matter of five or six hours, a team in an assortment of trucks had descended on the front lawn and put together this intricate structure. In about the same time, presumably the next morning, the same team would dismantle everything and take it away somewhere else and repeat the whole operation. He wondered what it had cost AgriBus to have this monster installed for, at most, an hour of use. Presumably, whoever had made the decision thought it was worth it. He also wondered what the videos were for. After all, whoever stood at the lectern would be easily seen from anywhere in the marquee, and would certainly be heard. Maybe the videos were to screen a prepared message from some distant authority figure at Helm & Hathaway who was too busy to attend the relatively small takeover of the AgriBus Human Ethicals Division.

He stood perfectly still in the main entrance, his eyes, now accustomed to the gloom, sweeping over the inside of the marquee. He smiled to himself as he suddenly realized he had made the somewhat humorous connection between the marquee and a circus. His imagination caught the theme. At four o'clock in the afternoon, a circus-like performance would begin in this marquee, with bulls and bears, daredevil rides, a little magic, speeches and music, and lots of clapping and cheering as the various performers went through their acts. And the employees of HED would go home for the weekend, streaming out of the marquee, pushing and jostling, having seen an amazing array of feats from highly professional and accomplished artists.

He was determined to watch the performance in a detached, even a scientific way, to see how it was done. He knew he would not be disappointed with the artistry of the performers in creating these illusions. It would make for an interesting 'four-square barbecue' on Sunday at his home. The three musketeers and their partners were coming. No children again, for the first time. They always had a barbecue on that first Sunday after they had been away to the beach, to work out who still owed what to whom. The four-squaring of accounts, Gloria Johns had once called it, and the label had stuck ever since. He had no doubt there would be plenty of heated discussion to go with the charcoal and the chilli sauce.

He felt a gentle tap on the shoulder. He looked around and saw Paul Ruffin standing behind him with that warm smile he knew Paul had been cultivating since his high school days.

"I thought I'd take a quick look at the set-up before the meeting this afternoon while I had this place all to myself. A bit like old times. You were always a step or two ahead of me then. How are you, Brian? It's been quite a while."

Brian seized Paul's outstretched hand enthusiastically. "Paul, it's good to see you again. I was wondering if you'd be here in some official capacity. And thank you for being so open with me over the phone the other day. Had to make sure the rumour was not a rumour. I greatly appreciated it." He waved his arm around. "An impressive set-up. Your doing?" he asked.

"Actually, no, Brian. It was your chairman, Charles Winton, who insisted the troops be brought together and the announcement made in joint statements. So we stuck him with the bill for this affair. Not cheap, you know, but he seemed quite happy to pay. He apparently said it was the least he could do for his people in HED. If it had been up to us at H & H, we would have done it differently. We're not much into speeches on occasions like this."

Brian nodded. "I've always liked Winton, and I'm not surprised he insisted on speaking personally to the staff. He had a lot to do with putting the division together about twelve years ago. It was one of his pet projects, running agri and human research side by side, each feeding off the other. Incidentally, just to return for a moment to your statement that you would have done it differently. What would you have done?"

Paul Ruffin hesitated. "Without going into the fine detail, we would have started talking to groups at the top, slowly working our way down, so as to better understand what made the new acquisition tick, and meanwhile feeding the rumour mill with what we wanted people to know. No sudden changes of direction, business as usual, until we knew precisely what needed to be done. In other words, no fanfare, no promises up front . . . until we were quite ready to integrate the new acquisition into our organization. I expect there would eventually have to be some downsizing in certain areas, but we would be very conscious of the fact that we were buying good people as well as a host of other physical assets. In a nutshell, that's about it."

"Interesting procedure, Paul. We'll wait and see how things work out. Is your chairman going to be here? What's his name? Italian sounding."

"Claudio Agostino, except that he's Brazilian. He won't be here today which is a pity. He puts on a great show. But we have his videotaped message welcoming AgriBus people into the H & H family, so to speak. He's away overseas. A long-term engagement, I've been told. So it will be the job of the deputy chairman, Mike Sandison, to represent H & H and reassure the AgriBus people it's going to be business as usual. Anyway, enough shop talk. How are Gretl and Kimmy? It's been ages since I last saw them. Kimmy must be quite a grown up young lady. All of sixteen, if I remember. How am I doing?"

"I'm impressed, Paul. You always were good at remembering such details. I haven't changed. I remember Mary's name but, for the life of me, I can't remember how many children you have."

"That's easy, Brian. None. Been too busy, Mary and I." They both laughed.

"How about a cup of coffee. We can have it in my office?"

"I really don't have the time, Brian. I have a breakfast meeting with your chairman and his team, and our deputy chairman and his team, in the AgriBus boardroom. There are some details still to be worked out – who goes first, who introduces who, matters of protocol."

"What part will you be playing in all this?"

"Unless some dramatic changes have taken place in the last twenty-four hours, I'm earmarked to be your new divisional general manager. And, may I add, Brian, if many of the people in the division are like you, being the boss will be a piece of cake. Let me tell you, I'll be looking for your advice and support." He took one more look around the inside of the marquee. "That will do well. Nothing but the best from you AgriBus people. I must go. Can't keep the big boys waiting. Great to see you again, Brian. Love to Gretl. We must all get together very soon, old friend. Mary is staying put for the time being. Her PR business, you know. I shall move into digs around here. Someone at AgriBus is taking care of that matter, but I'll be looking for a home-cooked meal every so often from my good friends." He shook Brian's hand hard, flashed that warm smile, and quickly went through the entrance to the marquee and back to his car outside the front of the building.

Brian followed him out. Paul's car, an expensive Jaguar, pulled quietly away from the curb, cutting without hesitation onto the narrow and relatively well-hidden minor road leading to the underground garage of the imposing AgriBus International head office. He already knows his way around, Brian thought. Always did do his homework very carefully. It was to be expected of course that Paul would run into him sometime and ask him about his family. Yet, he reflected, Kimmy was still a baby when Paul had last seen her and then only fleetingly. Therefore he would have made sure that Mary found out as much as possible through her contacts about each of the senior managers at AgriBus before he came down here. She was good that way; ambitious like Paul, and knew how to charm his bosses. The head of a small and quite profitable public relations firm, she was also excellent at her job. Well, Brian concluded, when push came to shove, Paul Ruffin would look after number one. He always had, both at university and obviously at H & H. He would be on the platform this afternoon, being introduced as their incoming general manager. It would be interesting to see how he went about easing himself into HED and how soon he decided who to ease out.

He went up the stairs leading to the front entrance of the building. He hadn't expected to run into anyone at this early hour, let alone Paul Ruffin. The new boss? This could turn out to be one of the more important days of his life. It would be good to have some influence where it mattered. With Paul Ruffin? Miracles happened every so often! He would find out soon enough.

Chapter 7

4.00 p.m., Friday, 3 January

The musketeers had come in early and settled for seats at the back of the marquee. This would give them a good view of the procession of dignitaries coming through the main entrance. They didn't need front row seats. They would hear what was said well enough, and they'd be able to leave the marquee relatively quickly when it was over. Looking around, Brian could see that just about everyone in the division was there. Even Colin Marks, the Marketing manager, who was not due back till the following Monday, had come in. Someone must have phoned him. Colin had waved to him when he had come into the marquee, a circling motion of both his hands indicating big things were in the wind. There was an attractive and professionally printed programme on each of the seats. It consisted of a list of the speakers and who they were. The organizers had even tried to put a time frame on each of the speakers so that everyone would know roughly when the meeting would be over. This general meeting was being done with all the trimmings, Brian thought. Good old Winton. He was going to do this right and, in the process, show the H & H mob that AgriBus cared about its people, even if they were about to sell them down the river!

The programme was quite straightforward. The chairman of AgriBus, Charles Winton, was to open the meeting, and was scheduled to speak for twenty minutes. No doubt he would go to some lengths to explain to everyone why HED had been sold to H & H. He was to be followed by Mike Sandison, deputy chairman of H & H, who would explain why Claudio Agostino, his chairman, was not there in person. However, the absent chairman had taped a short speech of welcome to the H & H family, which was the third item on the programme. Mike Sandison would comment on the chairman's message, emphasizing some of the points raised by his boss. Between them, that would take up another twenty minutes. Then Norman Coles, the AgriBus outgoing general manager, would introduce Paul Ruffin and say a few words, probably about handing over the baton and how closely they were going to work together to minimize takeover glitches – five minutes. Then came Paul Ruffin, a further five minutes, followed by ten minutes allotted to "question time". And finally Charles Winton was to close the meeting with a few well-chosen words. In all, about an hour. He had to admit, he could not have done better himself had he been in Winton's shoes.

Brian looked at his wristwatch. Four o'clock. There was a slight turning of heads and shuffling of feet near the entrance. They were forming up, he guessed, like an academic procession. He wondered if they would be wearing anything over their Fifth Avenue suits. Neon haloes, he thought, very bright and very pure, to accentuate their impeccable motives.

Britt, who was sitting on Brian's right, between him and Armand, with Tony on Brian's left, nudged Brian sharply in the ribs. In spite of her pneumatic form, she had the sharpest and boniest elbows of anyone he had ever known. "This is very good. They are on time, so they must know what they are doing, no?"

Brian had never told Britt that this jabbing in the ribs was quite painful at times. He casually wondered if she employed the same tactics with Ron every time she wanted to attract his attention. To get his own back, he simply looked at her and shrugged, which, he knew, annoyed her. She had told him often enough that she wanted a verbal rather than a non-verbal response to her queries. Too bad!

Britt glared back at him.

"Later, Beebee. Here they come," he told her.

The procession, in single file since the aisle was too narrow for two people to walk side by side, was led by the AgriBus chairman, Charles Winton, who walked through briskly and looking straight ahead, a picture of business-like determination as befitted the leader of a very large corporation doing his job, whatever the personal cost. He was followed closely by Mike Sandison, the deputy chairman of H & H, nodding and smiling benignly at the people on both sides of the aisle, reassuring, friendly, and distinctly giving the impression that ahead of him lay the pleasant duty of inviting all these excellent people to join him in making his company even greater than it already was. Then there was a small, respectful gap of a few yards. The next person was a woman whom Brian had never seen before. Who was she?

As if in response to that unasked question, Tony bent sideways to whisper in his ear. "Roberta Harding, H & H's senior corporate lawyer. A real dragon."

Brian looked at her back as she followed the two CEOs down the aisle. Short and square, with little shape to her body, hair cut short, on flat-heeled shoes, a dark grey pant suit suitable for wearing on an elevated platform, no earrings or adornment of any kind. Probably in her early forties, probably with H & H for many years, maybe even her only job. The type who lived for her work and was very good at it. Completely professional, she would have trained her bosses never to do anything or go anywhere without knowing exactly what the legal implications were likely to be, and preferably always having her there to cover their backs. Never married, no children, a low set house in a fashionable suburb, a cleaning service once a week, good taste in furniture, paintings and Persian rugs. Enjoyed cooking, when she had an early evening at home. Also enjoyed travelling, but only on guided tours. Sometimes took a poor relation along, and there were lots of them; brothers, sisters, nephews, nieces, all of whom adored their aunt Roberta . . .

His line of vision, and his imagination, to which he had just given free rein on the subject of Roberta, was blocked by a young man, tall, very serious and good-looking, who was carrying a portable overhead projector together with a manila folder that almost certainly contained transparencies. Probably from Human Resources management, he would operate the overhead projector and put transparencies on the viewing panel at the nod of the speakers and, when it was all over, make sure nothing had been left behind. Another little gap in the procession. And then Paul Ruffin, wearing his warm smile, and Norman Coles last of all, trying not to look like a dispossessed division general manager but not succeeding, his eyes focused on the back of Paul Ruffin's tan shoes.

A moment later, they were all on the stage, waiting for a signal from Charles Winton to sit down on the chairs arranged on either side of the lectern. From left to right, Coles, Ruffin, empty chair for Winton, lectern, Sandison, Harding, spare chair. The young Human Resources manager was at the foot of the platform setting up the overhead projector on a long table and spreading out transparencies in some prearranged order. They were almost ready to start. Winton nodded to his right and left. The dignitaries sat down, collectively smiling at the sea of faces. Brian had been on platforms from time to time. In subsequent discussions with other dignitaries, he had found this was the most awkward moment for them, sitting down and facing the audience for the first time without appearing self-conscious or superior, perhaps frightened they might stumble in some way and make fools of themselves.

Charles Winton need not have cleared his throat to capture the attention of the HED employees. You could have heard a pin drop. The moment of truth was upon them. Not that anyone in the marquee had doubts about the content of the message. Like the audience at a Sophoclean tragedy, it was the way the message would be delivered that concerned them most. They had bought their admission ticket to this meeting by dint of hard labour, years of service, loyalty, all these good things, and now they wanted the full value of that ticket. They wanted to know the depth of the betrayal, the extent of the cupidity and greed of the protagonists. They wanted to get some measure of the lie. The atmosphere was palpable. Winton must surely feel it, Brian thought. Britt gave him this time a very gentle nudge in the ribs. So she must be feeling it too. He looked at Tony, at Armand. They were also caught up in the drama. Everyone in the marquee was. What a powerful moment for the performers on the stage. Now let the circus begin!

Chapter 8

3.30 p.m., Sunday, 5 January

The coals were dying in the barbecue. The sun had passed its zenith and the air was oppressively still, if a little chilly, in the sheltered patio. What remained of lunch had been cleared away from the long wooden table and the musketeers were looking thoughtfully at their mugs of steaming coffee and, in varying degrees, wondering what effect the huge slice of Black Forest gateau, courtesy of Britt Berghoff, would have on their cholesterol levels. The lovely Britt at her best again. She was determined, she told them without apology, that they should all end up like the father she remembered and adored, a man of considerable substance. She was succeeding beyond her wildest dreams, they assured her, contemplating the slice of cake before them.

"OK," Gretl said. "Now that we've settled the four-square accounts, would it be appropriate to find out what actually happened on Friday afternoon at that meeting? Let's do it carefully and completely. I know what Brian told me, in a disjointed sort of way. But this is too important to all of us not to try and understand what came out. So let's start at the beginning. I have

Brian's copy of the programme," straightening out the folds in the sheet in front of her. "Charles Winton opened the proceedings. What did he say and, more importantly, what did it mean?" She sat back in her yellow director's chair and waited.

Tony shrugged. "The message was clear to me. H & H bought the division because, would you believe, they want the building and the equipment in it. Which makes most, if not all of us, redundant . . ."

"*Un moment, mon ami,*" Armand interrupted. "That is not what I heard Winton say, or any of the others. *Mais oui*, they want our building, which is perfect for pure research and development with all its laboratories, space for experimental animals, and so forth. To replicate everything we have would cost them a lot more if they tried to do it today, so it is a very good investment for them. But both Sandison and Ruffin were quite clear. They want us to continue as we are, but with a slightly different focus, which is to be expected."

"This is not what I heard from all their talking," Britt said, her mouth half-full of gateau. She held up her hand as she tried to hurry her swallowing and began to cough instead.

"You're going to choke and then give yourself indigestion, pet," Ron told her, rubbing her back, gently.

Catching her breath once again, Britt lowered her arm. "OK. I stop eating, darling, while I talk. I think both of you are a little right. *I* know what they are going to do with the division. Yes, they want the building. Yes, they want to keep us working, maybe on different things. But I think they have one very special product they want to develop, something for AIDS, the prostate, it doesn't matter. I think it is something very hush-hush, and they want to hide it among a bunch of people who are not likely to understand what is going on. What better place than AgriBus. That is what I think."

Armand was quick to rebut. "Rubbish, Beebee. One product? The building was not designed for researching one product, or even two. It was designed for small groups of scientists to work together on a whole group of different drugs. The lucky break is all that AgriBus needed. Well, it has not worked out that way. No lucky breaks, not soon enough for them, nor for us. And now everyone looks for all sorts of dark reasons why they are doing this takeover thing, which is stupid. I think it is just a very good investment for H & H. I think the directors of AgriBus have been trying to get rid of HED for some years and they have probably given it away to H & H for a song. It was an interesting experiment for Winton and a few others years ago. Now it is all over for them. I think H & H will just add our operation to their other operations, they will push us into areas where they have good markets and most of us will keep our jobs and continue doing what we are doing now. I welcome this takeover, and you should also, Beebee. It will mean increased opportunities for doing better, maybe even more important research. They know the current horizons of human ethical research and they will give us the support we need to develop and do interesting things. What do you think, Brian?"

Brian became very conscious of being stared at by everyone around the table. They were asking D'Artagnan to wave his magic sword and pluck the truth out of the air. He didn't know any more about the H & H plans for the division than any of them. Paul Ruffin had not offered any such information on the phone or during their chance meeting in the marquee that morning. All they could do, it seemed, was to try and define any special meaning there might have been in what each of the speakers had said. Getting four minds to recall what had been said might just yield some implied reason for the takeover and some direction for the future. Certainly, it would be more productive than these blanket conclusions which had just been proposed.

"I'm not sure this will provide any answers, but I think we should try and recall what each of the speakers said and see if we can deduce what H & H intend to do with HED. I suppose we should start with Charles Winton." He looked at the other three for confirmation.

Gloria immediately concurred. "I think that's an excellent

idea. I know Tony came home depressed by what he'd heard and spent a good part of yesterday updating his CV."

Once again Brian felt they were expecting him to play conductor – draw out the best from each instrument, follow through on the main themes, and reach conclusions with a crashing, logical crescendo. This was not a leadership position he relished, but who else? It had always seemed that way, for all the years they had been friends. When they wanted someone to engage in conflict resolution, they turned to him. So he would give direction. "Tony, why don't you kick things off and tell us what you most recall Winton saying?"

Tony thought for a moment. "If we ignore the industry graphs and figures, which I expect a lot of the other people found interesting but which I would think all of us already knew, it wasn't until he began to break out AgriBus's profitability by division that I began to get a sense of direction. He was telling us HED wasn't providing the ROI the shareholders were expecting, and by shareholders, he pointed the finger at the institutions who own a significant proportion of the corporation. He also said HED never would meet ROI expectations without a significant injection of money and a long-term commitment to research."

"That is absolutely correct," Britt interjected. "I think Winton was very open when he explained that the initial decision to move into human ethicals was a good fifteen years ago. Now the pharmaceutical industry has changed. There has been a lot of consolidation because of the cost of research. It was Agostino who reminded us it cost well over one hundred million pounds and ten years of work to bring out one new drug. Inventing a new cure was the least of it. There was always the possibility another company would beat them to the punch and discover something similar, or there would be some side effect on consumers and a class action would ruin the company, as had happened to a number of other companies over the last ten years or so. So, the industry is very risky."

"It isn't as if we didn't recognize these issues," Tony added morosely. “I expect most of us in the industry are aware of them. The bottom line is that Winton was telling us indirectly what had been discussed at board level, namely, either throw a lot more cash into HED or get out. He was also telling us the decision was not purely the board’s. It had to do with the investors, mainly the institutions, who were looking for greater stability in investment decisions and would respond negatively to a decision to get away from fundamentals – agricultural products.”

Gretl held up her hand. “Does this cover Winton’s talk? Was he only interested in telling you why the decision was taken to sell out? Did he say anything about H & H and why sell to them? Did he say anything about the intentions of H & H?”

There was a moment of silence as the musketeers considered her questions. It fell to Brian to reply. “That pretty well covers Winton, I think. He was trying to tell us that there were a number of factors to be considered: first, as much as they had no regrets at the initial decision to invest in human ethicals, the industry has changed over the last fifteen years; second, AgriBus would have to make a significant investment if it wanted to stay in the human ethicals game; and third, the institutions were telling them to get back to fundamentals and not throw any more money into that bottomless pit. As I recall, he mentioned H & H at the very end, but only to hand over to Sandison. Incidentally, I think it was right and proper he should leave it to the H & H people to explain who they were and what they had in mind as the buyers.”

Gretl once again held her hand in the air. “That covers Winton. How about Sandison?” she asked of no one in particular, and looking hard at the programme.

Brian shrugged and looked at Armand. “Armand, I think Sandison is yours.”

“Ah, yes. I found Sandison very interesting. It is not what he said, but rather what he did not say. First, he says he will show us the video of his boss, Agostino, after making apologies for his not being able to be there. And then he picks on three points that Agostino makes. Initially, he emphasizes the big growth of H & H over the last ten years and some of the very successful drugs they have put on the market. In other words, we will be part of a very large and powerful company in our own industry. But he says nothing about H & H being mostly in the over-the-counter business. He wants to make it sound as if they are big time in pure research. Next he talks about the emphasis on heart research and some new areas of increasing interest. And finally he talks about people and how they are their most important asset. Where have I heard all that before, *hein*!"

"What are you trying to say, *mon chéri*?" Michelle asked her husband.

"They have huge resources, H & H. They have laboratories all over the world. Why come to our little division for hush-hush work? It does not make any sense, Michelle. It is all very simple. I think AgriBus want to sell. I think H & H want to buy. The price is right. It is good business. *Voilà*. End of story."

"Armand may be right, Michelle. In any case, I don't think we'll get any further along by arguing about it. Any other thoughts on Sandison?" Brian waited a moment or two. "Let me say I know about some of the conditions of employment H & H have. They're a very good company to work for, every bit as good as AgriBus, maybe even better. Anyway, could Agostino have given us a clue about the reasons for the takeover? Beebee, what did you get out of his video?"

"It seemed to me he tried only to sell H & H to us. He wanted us to believe the takeover was something we should welcome. He started by telling us what a great company H & H is. It had done many good things and we should all be very happy to become part of his company. Then he went on to describe the future of the company, a future limited only by the good efforts of its employees. Then he asked us to consider the prospects of working in a company with the resources of H & H. For example, if you are a scientist, if you have a good idea, they will let you run with it as far as you want to go, whatever it costs. It was all very positive, I thought."

Tony nodded. "No question. If you're one of the few who will be kept on, you should do very well. Sandison didn't say much about the working conditions and remuneration package. Like Brian, though, I've heard good reports of them. But I've also heard that they tend to be ruthless when they have to be, particularly with people who are disloyal or don't pull their weight. I appreciate what a risk Paul Ruffin was taking when he told you the takeover was on, Brian. If that had got out, he would not have been sitting on that platform."

Brian leaned forward. "Talking of Paul Ruffin, shall we pass on to him? I think we've probably exhausted what Agostino said in his message. By the sound of his remarks, Paul was trying to be positive, upbeat, non-threatening in any way. Have I got it right? Armand, you have said very little for a while."

"I think everyone is right about Agostino. He wanted to reassure us. As for Paul Ruffin, he is your friend, Brian. You should talk about him, not me."

Brian waited for a moment, looking around the table. There seemed to be general agreement that he should attempt to analyse Paul Ruffin's very brief speech and possibly offer some impressions about him based on their past friendship. "It appeared to me that, like the other H & H people, Sandison and Agostino, Paul was backpedalling furiously, being too conciliatory, being very careful not to give the impression that he intended to make changes quickly. The last thing he wanted was to leave the employees of HED with the impression that they would be retired or fired, that their jobs would be changed dramatically, that arbitrary transfers would take place, that sort of thing. It didn't come out of his mouth, but you could sense it from his general demeanour and body language."

"I've known him for a long time. He's very hard indeed to pin down, to define – rather like a chameleon. He seemed to be trying hard to be open, saying how he was looking forward to working with poor old Norman, who couldn't hide his misery. Norman would have been much happier if Winton had announced that he would work with the H & H people until they were comfortable taking over, and then he would revert back to AgriBus to move into some bigger and better job. Winton said nothing. I suspect part of the deal is that Norman Coles, Colin Marks, maybe even Julian Horne and Karl Helmreich, our revered bosses, Armand, will all receive golden handshakes, but only after they have divulged all their knowledge on HED to Paul and his mob. I give them another two to three months and by then at least two of them will be gone. Did Paul say anything that might suggest something special was ahead for HED? The answer is no. He stuck to the party line throughout, with Norman nodding at appropriate moments. I feel sorry for Norman. He plays a good political game, but he was out of his league with that lot."

Gretl and Britt spoke almost in unison, as they tended to do from time to time. "So where does this leave us, Brian?"

Brian shrugged in his characteristic way. "I haven't a clue. Are we any further towards knowing what is likely to happen to HED? My feeling is that H & H probably don't know either. My guess is that Armand was absolutely right. AgriBus wanted to sell, and H & H decided to buy because it was too good a deal to pass by. Now they have to decide how best to use the people and the facilities. I also think they have no intention of moving precipitously. They won't be firing anyone until they have some very clear idea of where they want to go. The first indication of that will be when any of our leaders moves out of his office and is escorted to his car with a couple of boxes in his arms. Then things will begin to happen fast."

"So we have at least one month, maybe two months at most," Tony cut in. "I guess I'd better get moving and find another job."

Gloria shook her head. "Darling, take it quietly. There's no immediate rush for anyone in HED to do anything quickly. Let's wait and see. Yes, begin exploring alternatives, a phone call here, a visit there, all quiet. Paul Ruffin would expect some of that to happen and, if he finds out you're looking outside and he doesn't try to stop you, then you'll know he would prefer you to find your own job rather than be pushed out, and he'll give you a bit of time, I'm sure."

"Spot on," Brian supported her. "We should all have a quiet look around, see what's out there, just in case. If we happen to find something about the same but secure, we make our move. Then it's up to H & H to tell us what they have in mind for the long term. In those circumstances, we can always decide to stay, and we would do that from a position of strength. Well, people, I've had it. I'm suddenly tired. I think we should watch what's left of the football on the box. Who's with me? Bring your coffee and cake and let's push the kids out of the way."

Part III

Changes at the top

Chapter 9

10.00 a.m., Monday, 6 January

Brian looked around the crowded boardroom. He had always liked this room. It had originally been intended as a meeting place for any senior executive wishing to get together with ten or more people, as scientists and sales people often did. However, Norman Coles had used his executive power as general manager of the division to have a door knocked through to his corner office and had insisted that the room be used only with his approval. Effectively, it had become an extension of his office and had been unofficially designated the boardroom HED – which meant it was not only aptly named but, more importantly, grossly underutilized.

It could comfortably seat twenty people around the six tables which, when joined together, formed a single large rectangle. At some point soon after Coles's expropriation, a bar had been added at the farthest end away from the connecting door, complete with double sink and hot and cold running water. That little exercise, Brian and others in the division thought, must have cost a pretty penny. Although no comment was ever made, they were sure it had come out of the division budget under the heading of "modifications to a laboratory". Norman Coles had also installed a good-sized refrigerator and two coffee machines, one of which made the espresso coffee that he himself drank almost continuously.

On the rare occasions when Brian had been to meetings in the boardroom, he had been impressed by the elegance of the cream panelled walls, the quality burgundy carpet, and the glossy wooden tables and leather chairs. But that congenial atmosphere was considerably marred by cheaply framed photographs of past AgriBus CEOs along both side walls. One of the consolations of the takeover was his fond hope Paul Ruffin would have these offending pictures removed and replace them with landscapes. For that matter, almost anything would be better than Charles Winton and his stern-faced predecessors staring down their noses at the proceedings.

All the managerial staff appeared to be present, a few standing at the bar, styrofoam cups of coffee in their hands, the remainder sitting at the table chatting quietly to their neighbours as they waited for something to happen. Predictably, people from the same divisional departments sat together. Sales and Marketing were clustered at the far end of the table, Research along one side, Development on the other. The two exceptions were the musketeers and the three department managers: Colin Marks, Karl Helmreich and Julian Horne. These three sat together closest to the head of the table, presumably because they felt they should reflect the seniority of their positions by being nearest the seat of power. Brian had chosen to sit opposite them because he wanted to see Paul Ruffin perform at close range. He wanted to miss nothing. He had forewarned his fellow musketeers and they had assured him they would be right there with him. They also wanted a ringside seat, but for different reasons; Armand and Britt because they wanted an unimpeded view of Norman Coles squirming, Tony because he was determined to ask at least one question about job security and didn't want to be overlooked.

Paul Ruffin and Norman Coles came through the connecting

door from Norman Coles's office just as the clock struck ten. Paul had always prided himself on being punctual, so Brian wasn't surprised. The executives at the bar quickly resumed their seats as Norman Coles sat down in one of the two vacant chairs at the head of the table. He placed a pad and pen carefully before him, and sat back in his chair staring uncomfortably at the ceiling. Being relegated to a secondary role before his erstwhile subordinates evidently sat badly on his narrow shoulders. Paul Ruffin, on the other hand, remained standing behind his chair, wearing his warmest smile. He was enjoying his moment of power.

Paul's eyes wandered quickly around the table, taking in the presence of only two women on the managerial staff. For a moment, Paul dropped his smile and pursed his thin lips. He didn't like that, Brian thought, reading his mind. What more noticeable initiative than to increase significantly the number of women executives among the twenty or so people who headed the various sections and departments. And he probably knew exactly where to find them in H & H and how to entice them over. Pointedly looking at Britt and Amanda Fowler, a senior biochemist in Research, he leaned forward, supporting himself on the back of the chair.

"Ladies", he emphasized, looking at Amanda and then Britt, "and gentlemen. Thank you all for attending this meeting at such short notice. Let me make one thing perfectly clear before we go any further. These pictures have got to go!" He waved at the dozen or so pictures on the walls, a broad grin on his face.

There was a moment of silence as the irrelevance of his opening statement as the new divisional general manager sank in. Amanda Fowler was the first to giggle and that was followed by an uproarious laugh as everyone in the room joined in. A few of the Sales people even clapped their approval. Paul Ruffin had just scored a victory, and he knew it, even if it had been at Norman Coles's expense. But then, there was no one in the room who felt especially sorry for their former boss, certainly not over the HED boardroom.

Brian waited for Paul to milk that situation. He expected him to ask whether there was any objection to his proposal, or suggest that everyone who approved hold up both their hands and wave them around, or some such thing. But he did not. Brian had to admire the man's style. That was a very clever opening gambit and he apparently wasn't going to overdo it.

He sneaked a look at Norman Coles, who continued to look fixedly at the ceiling as if none of this had happened. Brian, however, knew Norman Coles well, and he was sure that Paul Ruffin had just made an implacable enemy. He wondered if Paul was aware of this, if this had in fact been one of his intentions. Knowing Paul's calculating mind, Brian guessed it would all have been very much part of Ruffin's planning: to bring a presumably suspicious, even antagonistic, group of highly skilled and intelligent executives onto his side with one astute gesture and, at the same time, demonstrate to the group that he was capable of being completely ruthless when he chose to be, even if it meant antagonizing his predecessor. So much for Paul Ruffin's highly effective grand opening!

Paul unhurriedly pulled his chair away from the table and sat down, his warm smile still on his face. "Well, people," he paused for effect, "let's get down to business. My name is Paul Ruffin. I've been appointed general manager of this division by the board of Helm & Hathaway. Some of you already know me and, in Brian Curtis's case, he has known me since our university days when we shared an apartment for two years. It's great to have old friends on my team." He leaned over and patted Brian's arm.

"I hope you will bear with me. Who am I? I have a Ph.D. in veterinary pathology. I've been with H & H for some sixteen years, the last four as the manager of animal pathology at their central laboratories. I'm married, no children. My wife is in public relations and I expect we'll be commuting a lot for the next few months." He shrugged. "The price of upward mobility in the corporate world. I want you all to know I'm truly looking forward to this assignment and I'll be relying on your total support if we're going to get the job done successfully."

Tony Johns' hand shot up. "What is your assignment?"

"A direct question deserves a direct answer. My job is to integrate the HED division of AgriBus into the worldwide research and development activities of H & H as rapidly as possible." Paul waited.

Another hand shot up at the other end of the table. "Does this mean you won't need the marketing group?"

Paul smiled his warm smile. "Not at all. Just because I didn't mention Sales or Marketing doesn't mean you won't be needed. On the contrary, we'll need your expertise more than ever. Before we go off on all sorts of tangents, let me make sure you all understand what we, at H & H, mean by 'integrate'. We've done this takeover thing a few times over the last ten or fifteen years, as all of you probably know. Each time we go through a takeover, we get better at it. But we also continue to make mistakes because we don't ever fully understand what's going on. Let me give you an example. Who do you go to when you want to get something done? If you follow the established reporting relationships and lines of communication, it doesn't take any time at all to know who you have to go to. But you know, and I know, that's not the way things get done. You have to find out who *not* to go to when you want to get something done, and that can take a long time, if ever. I'm talking about the formal versus the informal, organization, what's on paper and what's never put down on paper but, somehow, over the years, you learn by osmosis, you learn where the traps are." Paul waited for this to sink in. "What I'm saying is that, each time we go through a takeover, we are dealing with a distinctly different corporate culture that has taken years to develop, and we have to learn what that is as quickly as we can before we start making decisions, or we're likely to make serious and costly mistakes."

Paul looked carefully around the table. He could see they understood that he was leading them down a well-trodden path and they wanted to see where that path would end and how it would affect them. He certainly had their attention. "As of 1st January, everything that was the AgriBus Human Ethicals Division, HED, is part of H & H. It's as if we've walked into a store and said to the checkout person, 'We'll have the lot. Not just your stock, but you and all your fellow workers at every level, these facilities, your technology, your accounting systems, your customers, your suppliers, your way of doing things.' By the lot, I mean everything. If you can put a name to it, if you can think of it, H & H will have to deal with it. And what makes it rather tricky is that we're going to have to take what we find here and work it into the H & H way of doing things without making an awful mess."

Paul looked around the table slowly, his face stern, his eyes flint hard. "If we could leave you to continue doing what you're doing now, it would be simple. And many takeovers are just like that: the organization taken over is left to get on with what it's been doing, quite often with top management left intact. But in this situation, we have to integrate you. That's because we've bought a piece of a company. As from 1st January, you're all on H & H's payroll. We have to transfer your accounts to our accounts. We have to continue paying your bills, supply your customers, a hundred and one different activities that have to be understood and integrated. For the next month or so, this is what I and a few others from H & H will be doing. And then, when things begin to work the way they do at H & H, we'll have to start making some hard decisions. There are bound to be a few things we can't use, a few people we don't need. And they will have to go. We try and make that separation as painless as possible, but there's nothing in any manual which makes a retrenchment enjoyable."

Paul sat back in his chair and shrugged. "All of you here this morning are being asked to do two things from this moment on. First, you must continue working as if nothing has happened. And you must make sure your subordinates at every level continue to work as always. It's critical we maintain momentum and morale. Second, you're asked to cooperate fully with the H & H people who will be going around trying to understand how things get done in HED. The sooner we integrate systems and procedures, the sooner we can work out how best to make use of your individual talents and tie you into H & H's continued activities and growth. Then we can all begin to contribute to the bottom line. This is my job for the next twelve months or so, ladies and gentlemen, and I propose to get it done as efficiently and effectively as I know how. And now, over to you. If you have any questions, this is as good a time as any to have them answered."

Brian had to give Paul due credit. He had laid out the plan for them, he had been as forthright as anyone could wish, and he appeared to want to play the game straight down the middle. He had left them with no illusions that continuing to work in the H & H equivalent of HED would not entail change. How substantial that change would be and how it would affect each of them, no one could say at present, least of all Paul Ruffin. But there would be change, nothing was more certain. It would be an interesting year!

Brian half raised his hand. "I'd like to know why H & H acquired the AgriBus HED."

Paul nodded. "This was a question which was not addressed by either your chairman or ours at the general meeting last Friday. I think it should have been explained. The simple answer is that it made a lot of business sense. We always need first-class R&D facilities and scientists." He looked down the length of the table at the Sales and Marketing executives and gave them his warm smile. "We also always need the sales and distribution facilities of a competitor. We heard this operation was for sale. We made an offer, AgriBus accepted. They wanted to get out, we wanted to get in. That's the way it happened. It didn't happen quickly or painlessly. This deal was in the making for some months, at the highest corporate levels. Amazingly, nothing came out until bits of paper began floating around, and then the rumours started, as they always do. Then we had to move quickly, which we did. That's it, in a nutshell, Brian."

Paul gave them a full minute, calmly looking around the table. He had obviously covered the ground well. There were no other questions. "I expect there will be more questions at a later time. I want you to know that you can ask anything you like. My job is to answer your questions, and my door is always open. Thank you for your attention and I look forward to working with each of you over the coming weeks." He stood, nodded to Norman Coles, and together they made their way out of the room.

As the HED management people began to stand, stretch, share meaningful looks, Paul Ruffin returned to the room. "One last announcement, everyone. As of this moment, this room is available for meetings. Phone my secretary and let her know when you want it and for how long – only to avoid double bookings." And he went out once again.

Brian and the musketeers remained seated. So did the three department managers opposite. They waited for the room to clear. "A strong performance, Brian," Julian Horne, his boss, stated in his customary deadpan voice. "But then, you would have seen some of this over the years."

"The potential was always there, Julian. It was interesting to see it in full bloom. I was impressed."

Karl Helmreich shook his massive head up and down. "I think he will be an asset, that one," in his thick German accent. "I think he will give us the support we need to do our jobs. What do you say, Brian?"

"He's no pushover, Karl, never has been. He'll do whatever it takes to look after Paul Ruffin first, the division second, and the staff last of all. But if his future prospects are tied in to staff performance, then he'll be in there fighting alongside us, that I do know. What struck me most of all, however, was his ability to give us just enough, without divulging company secrets. I wanted to ask him what it had cost H & H to acquire the division, but I knew he wouldn't tell me. He'll wait till the announcement is made in the press, if it ever appears. Somehow, I think AgriBus would prefer to keep this quiet. It doesn't go well with our image." Brian paused briefly. "Oops! I'd better get used to being an H & H man. Well, I'm going back to work." He pushed his chair back and stood. Without a word, the other musketeers also rose and silently filed out of the room, leaving their three superiors having their first meeting in the newly liberated division boardroom.

Chapter 10
3.00 p.m., Friday, 10 January

Brian Curtis noticed with pleasure the portraits of the AgriBus chairmen had gone from the walls, even if the picture hooks were still there. Paul had apparently not decided whether he wanted to replace them with something more appropriate or whether he would have the hooks removed and the holes painted over. In any event, it had improved the atmosphere of the boardroom immeasurably.

Paul Ruffin brought the meeting to order. "Amanda and gentlemen, I believe you have met my two colleagues from H & H, John Trury and Isabel Esporanta. You might say that they're my right and left hands. They'll be with us at the HE Division for the foreseeable future. They're experts on how we do things at H & H and their task is to integrate your reporting and accounting procedures into the company information system. I've also taken the liberty of inviting your understudies in your departments to this meeting: Brian Curtis in Development, Amanda Fowler in Research and Dale Cummings in Marketing. I hope you agree with my selections."

Julian Horne raised his hand. "I have no trouble with your

choice of my understudy. But it raises two questions. Should you have consulted with me before you made your selection? Does it mean you're grooming Brian to replace me?"

"I was going to ask the same questions, Paul," Colin Marks added.

Karl Helmreich looked sideways at Amanda Fowler. "This is nothing personal, Amanda." He turned to Paul. "Had you consulted with me, Paul, I would have pushed for Armand Hernier. He's our most senior research scientist, he's been with us the longest and he would be my logical replacement if I were to leave for whatever reason."

Paul's warm smile disappeared. "Question one. Should I have consulted with you beforehand? I don't think so. When it comes to making decisions about people who report directly to me, I have to make that call myself. Then, if I've made a mistake, I can only blame my poor judgement, and not your advice. It also avoids the possibility of a conflict if you suggest someone else and I don't agree. I don't have to tell you, Karl, there are a whole set of factors involved in deciding who gets the nod and who doesn't. If it puts someone's nose out of joint, that's the way things go sometimes, and I'm prepared to live with that. As they say, it comes with the job. I hope that answers your first question."

He paused and looked at his senior executives one by one. There were no comments. "Next. Does it mean I'm grooming your subordinates for your positions? One of the decisions that H & H insist all executives make soon after they start in a new role is to propose who their most likely successor will be and to begin to train that person thoroughly in all the facets of their job. It serves a multiplicity of purposes. It means that if something happens to an executive, there is someone who can slide into that person's job with relatively little trauma. More importantly, it means that an executive can be moved or promoted because of a sudden need without leaving a significant hole in his or her organization. And most importantly, it ensures that all executives will have thought through what their jobs are about if they're able to impart that knowledge to a subordinate. There are a number of other reasons which I don't propose to go into. I think I've answered your two questions, Julian. Now let's press on."

Paul Ruffin opened a folder and glanced hurriedly through some notes. Brian noticed that his customary warm smile was not present. They were about to see the real Paul Ruffin in operation. "We'll meet every Friday in this boardroom at three in the afternoon from now onwards until further notice. These meetings are, at the most basic level, an attempt to review what has been achieved during that week and to plan what we should be doing for the next one. I will naturally be meeting with some, or most of you, during the week, but it is the weekly Friday meeting which I want you to consider absolutely sacrosanct. It's the time when we tell each other what's been going on in our departments and decide how best to move the whole operation forward without making too many mistakes. I appreciate one or two of you may have to be elsewhere on business on any given Friday, but one or the other, preferably both, from each department must be present to report. In a sense, you may think of the nine of us as the board of the HE Division. Talking of which, I would prefer we use HE Division rather than HED from now on. This organization is not a nautical lavatory. It is a collection of very capable individuals who have a significant contribution to make, not only to H & H's bottom line, but also to medical science. I hope this makes sense. I'm proud to lead such a distinguished group of people. I also want you all to feel as good about being part of the HE Division as I do. Any questions?"

Brian raised his hand. "I can understand the rationale behind the inclusion of those present here today. But there may be one or two others who provide vital support to the division who should be part of the decision-making process."

"For example?" Paul asked.

"Tony Johns, our regulatory affairs director for one. He has saved us too many times to recount from going in directions which would have landed us into all sorts of trouble. I believe he should be part of any decision-making group such as this."

"Point taken. Let me think about this. Anyone else, Brian?"

"Norman Coles?"

"I understand your concern about the absence of your former boss, but this is my executive team and I'm anxious to establish my way of doing things, as well as my credibility. I don't think having my predecessor present would be helpful." Paul looked around the table expectantly. "In that case, if there are no more questions, let's get on with my agenda. There are three activities on which I want us all to focus over the coming weeks.

"First, I want the six of you, obviously the pairs in each of the three departments, to prepare a report in which you explain what you've been doing for the last twelve months and what you project you will be doing for the next six months. Norman tells me you have plans that go out ten years, so it should not be too difficult to get these reports ready. And keep them concise, no more than ten pages. If, by any chance, there is disagreement over any part of that report between any two of you, you should see this as a great opportunity for vigorous discussion and have the disagreement recorded so that we can all talk about it. I want you to be able to defend these activities. By this I mean that you should be able to justify to me, John and Isabel, that you have been and still are conducting economically viable activities. I want copies of these reports to each of us by 10.00 a.m. next Friday morning so that we can study them in time for our weekly meeting at 3.00 p.m. I would also like copies of your reports distributed to your fellow committee members. That way, we'll waste as little time as possible in catch-up activities during the meeting. Questions?"

Paul sat back in his chair and waited a full minute, his eyes going methodically from one face to another. "In that case, let's move on. Second, I want you to gather every form, every printed piece of paper, every computer program which you require in order to communicate with each other and elements outside the HE Division – not just AgriBus, but clients, suppliers, other research laboratories. As soon as you've done that, you are to contact John and Isabel and go through with them what each of these documents or programs does. They must understand clearly what it is you do, when, with whom, and why. The sooner they're completely familiar with how things get done, the sooner we can key you into the H & H information system, which is vast as well as highly sophisticated. Let me add one note of explanation. You may think us arrogant at H & H. That's partly true. We try to be the best in the pharmaceutical industry. We don't do this by ourselves. We learn constantly from other organizations, especially those we acquire, like yourselves. I would be very surprised if, at the end of this exercise, John and Isabel don't tell me that they much prefer the way a number of things get done in AgriBus or even just in the HE Division."

"This may take a little longer than a few days, Paul," Colin Marks remarked, looking at Dale Cummings for support. "What do you think, Dale?"

"We'll give it our best shot. Leave this one with me, Colin. I'll try to map out all the connections internally and externally. As long as you're comfortable with me pulling a few of our people together in a task force," Dale looked at Paul for confirmation.

"That's fine with me," Paul nodded. "I expect each department will have to put together a few heads to sort out everything that goes on. What I think we should plan is a formal presentation by John and Isabel, after you've gone through the information system in each of your departments with them. If they make mistakes during that presentation because there were things they didn't understand, that's great. It will mean that they can rectify those points and we will have the best possible chance of avoiding similar errors later when it will matter most. Any problems with my thinking?"

Once again Paul sat back in his chair and waited for comments from the group. He noticed Brian smiling. "What's going on in that head of yours, old friend? I remember you doing that when things were very bad or very good."

"You're doing just fine, Paul," Brian replied, the smile still on his face.

"I'm glad. I'm trying hard. OK, let's move on to my third and probably most sensitive requirement. I want you to prepare a list of all the people in your departments and make an assessment of their value to the HE Division. Unlike the first two activities, this third activity must be done by just the two of you in each department."

Julian Horne raised his hand hesitantly once again. "You want us to assess the value of every one of our people to the HE Division? Did you have any criteria which we can use to assess them?"

"I have some ideas, but I would prefer to talk about the criteria we might use, rather than specify them to you. Any suggestions?"

Karl Helmreich spoke out. "Education, length of service in the division, position, potential for promotion, that kind of thing?"

"Exactly," Paul replied.

"But even if we come up with an acceptable list of criteria, shouldn't we weight them or are they all equal in value?" Amanda Fowler asked.

It was Brian's turn. "So what if we do come up with an acceptable evaluation method, where does that take us? What we'll have is a list of people, many of whom do totally different jobs and have different values to the organization, depending on the scarcity of the job. Should we have a stab at determining how difficult it would be to replace any specific person? And then how long it takes us to induct the replacement into the culture of the organization so that they can find their way around? There are a few imponderables, Paul."

Paul Ruffin had subsided in his chair, his head resting on his chest. He said nothing for a while, then shrugged in resignation and stood up. "Somewhere along the line," he said, speaking to no one in particular, "there will be an initial reduction in work-force. Nothing is more certain. At the moment, I have no idea how many will have to go. It will depend on a number of factors, some to be decided at head office, some because certain skills will no longer be needed. What I'm trying to do is prepare for that eventuality. Having a list with what I call a *criticality* level against each name will enable us to start at the bottom of the list, counsel them on finding alternative employment, give them golden handshakes, that kind of thing. The process can be carried out slowly, with sensitivity, and hurting morale as little as possible."

He walked up and down the twelve or so feet of the width of the boardroom, his head still low on his chest, clearly not enjoying the message he was sharing with them. "I expect you already knew this would happen. I'm trying to establish a priority list: those we must do our best to retain, those who will have to go." He sat down and looked around the table. "If any of you have a better method for identifying both ends of this continuum, please speak up. Let me just add one last thought. We're not reinventing the wheel. This goes on all the time. Most often, decisions are made behind closed doors and retrenchment notices are issued to satisfy an arbitrary percentage reduction. Then individuals are informed that their services are no longer needed, security guards march them to their desks, their personal belongings are thrown in one or more boxes, they're escorted to their cars, their access cards and other identification is taken from them, and they're ordered off the company grounds never to be admitted again. We don't like doing things like that at H & H, but in the end it all boils down to the same requirement. There is an unpleasant job that has to be done; in our case, we're trying to do that job with as little risk and unhappiness as possible."

He stopped pacing the floor and looked squarely at his senior executives. "Questions? If not, let me hand over to John and Isabel. They want to expand on the kinds of things you should be considering when you go through the three activities we have to focus on over the next few weeks. They've been through an exercise like this a couple of times before, and you'll find they have a great deal to contribute. Thank you for your attention and I look forward to meeting with you again next Friday." He gathered his papers and went through the door into his office.

Chapter 11

11.45 a.m., Wednesday, 15 January

Armand Hernier rose from his desk and paced the floor once again. The report he had just completed rereading was very poor – badly structured, poorly expressed, a couple of the tabulations did not add up correctly, and so on. This was most unlike Amanda Fowler. Ever since she had joined them some four years ago, she had been meticulous about everything she did, and certainly she had never handed in anything like that before. Was it because Paul Ruffin had selected her to understudy Karl Helmreich and she was making some kind of a statement? To whom? To him? Why? Just because she was suddenly the number two person in Research didn't change the realities. He was in charge of this project and she was doing one piece of it. If Karl had wanted to put her in charge, he would simply have taken the project away from him and given it to her. But it still wouldn't have changed the need for her to write that report. After all, she had been working on this piece of the project for over six weeks and she owed it to him and the others to be completely professional.

There was a gentle knock on the door and in walked Amanda

Fowler, her habitual smile missing from behind her round and scholarly glasses. "Aha, *ma petite*," Armand exclaimed. "I was just thinking of you." He gestured at the report which lay open on his desk. "Did you write this, or did your cat?"

Amanda threw herself in a chair. She crossed her arms on her thin bosom and grimaced.

"I know," he continued, resuming his seat at his desk. "You have fallen in love and it is unrequited. He has given you one look and run away and you are desolated. You cannot think straight, and you do not care about your work any more. It is all very boring, *n'est-ce pas?* How close am I to the truth?"

"Nowhere near. You should know better," she replied, her eyes fixed on a stain in the carpet in front of her feet. "You asked me to update my work on this project, and you wanted it urgently. I made the mistake of asking one of my technicians to write it up and I told him to hand it in to you. I didn't get round to looking at it until just now." She held up her hand. "And don't ask me who wrote it up. I shan't tell you. It doesn't matter anyhow. I apologize. But there is something more important I want to talk about."

"More important than this mess because you choose a person badly? If you want to be a good manager, you must surround yourself with people to whom you can delegate work without having to check it, *non*?"

"Don't worry about it. It'll be in your hands, properly done, first thing tomorrow morning, even if I have to sit up half the night."

"That is not the point, madam. Anyway, you look as if you have been sitting up half the night already," Armand observed, his eyes going over her drawn face and bloodshot eyes.

"It's this business of being Karl's understudy. It's getting to me. You know I had nothing to do with it. Paul Ruffin called me into his office last Friday morning and told me he wanted me to take on the job. We would talk about a considerable salary increase in due course, and all that guff. Very flattering, Armand.

But I've already had it. Karl is pushing things at me and a lot of it is pretty unpleasant."

"So?" he asked her, raising one bushy eyebrow.

"Well, it's the last of the three activities Karl and I are working on that's disturbing me."

"Since I do not know what these three activities are, you will have to be a little more informative, *non*?" he continued, his eyebrow still cocked inquiringly.

"I'm not supposed to talk about it to anyone, but I think you should have been involved, whether Paul Ruffin likes it or not. He wants Karl and me to list all the people in the Research Department and put a criticality estimate against each name."

"Criticality? What is that?"

"We have to state the level of importance of each person to the department, on a scale of one to five. Anyone with a five we must do our best to keep."

"And people with a one or two?"

"You've got it. They go. Not only this, he also wants the eighty-odd people in the department distributed on a normal curve so that we have as many scores of one as we have scores of five. None of this business of finding the three or four people whom we should have fired years ago and giving them a one, and everybody else has a five."

"So soon, eh! He is not wasting any time."

"The way he put it at the meeting last Friday, it sounded very fair. Even after we had agreed on the criteria for determining the scores, it still seemed the best way to go, until Karl and I started deciding who would be a one or a two. You know how sometimes you and Karl and I and a few of the others throw our hands in the air and ask ourselves how we ever hired such and such a person. Well, I never had to decide how I would go about firing them. I've decided I don't like doing it. It's a bit like playing God. I haven't been able to sleep properly since I started working on that list. And Karl is making things a lot harder – he's even more distressed than I am. What makes it really difficult is that I have never had anything to do with some of the people, let alone know how well or badly they perform. And we have to make decisions without talking to their supervisors. Paul Ruffin thinks Karl and I should know everyone in the department well enough to make these decisions. This is crazy. And, as if this isn't bad enough, I'm being head-hunted by Crowley Pharmaceutical. They want me to take over their research lab as soon as I can decently get away from AgriBus or H & H, or whoever we work for these days."

"But this is excellent news, Amanda. Crowley are small, but they are very professional about their research. You will like them very much. I think it is a great opportunity for someone with your talents and in your position. As for the other business, Karl must make the decisions. He does know everyone in the department. Even if he does not know a few of them well enough, he has the personnel records in his office. Anyway, you should not lose any sleep over this. So, what else do you want to discuss?"

"That's enough, Armand. You make everything sound so simple. All I need to do is go and see Karl and tell him I'm resigning. And he will accept my resignation and a few weeks later, I'm at Crowley's, two hundred miles away, in charge of their research laboratory. And they pay for me to rent a house, have my furniture moved, put my house over here on the market, pay me for any losses I may have, give me a huge salary increase, and *voilà*, it is all done."

"That is precisely what you will do, unless you have rocks for brains. *Mais oui*, it is very simple. They want you, they make the arrangements. You sit back and enjoy the ride, as they say."

"Do you think Karl and Paul may want to keep me from going?"

"Even if they try, how can they give you such an opportunity? To be your own boss, that is very important. And then you will have to make decisions about the people who work for you. And you will not lose any sleep, I assure you. There is only you and the job. That is all that matters."

"But Karl is unhappy making the decisions?" she reminded him quietly, looking at him.

"Karl is not making the decisions because he wants to make them. He is being forced to make them, and he does not like it. Yes, he likes to be a boss, but he wants also to continue being a scientist. Which is why he would like you to make the hard decisions for him. This makes him feel that somehow he is not responsible. Well, that is not possible. He must wear two hats at the same time if he wants to continue to be the boss. And he cannot pass such matters on to Norman Coles any more. Anyway, you don't have to worry. You leave my office, you go to see Karl and you tell him you are accepting the research position with Crowley Laboratories. That is all. I think you are very lucky and you must take the bull by the horns when the bull is running with you. That is life, as they say."

Amanda Fowler continued to sit in her chair, her eyes still fixed on the stain in the carpet. She shook her head. "Armand, I'm grateful for your advice. This is a big move for me. If the H & H business hadn't come up, I don't think I'd be remotely interested in that offer. I'm just starting to feel good about my job. But now, somehow, things are different. Anyway, there's a lot to think about, even if you make it all sound so easy."

"But it is easy, Amanda," Armand emphasized. "The job is a great step forward for your career. You must at least give it serious consideration, *ma petite* . . ."

Armand was interrupted by a light knock on the door. Karl Helmreich put his head in. "There you are, Amanda. I thought I would find you with Armand. May I come in?" he asked, always very polite.

"Naturally, Karl. You are just in time, or maybe you are just a little ahead of time." He stood up and offered Karl the remaining chair in his office. "Amanda was talking to me about all sorts of interesting things that are happening to her."

Amanda frowned, her eyes still fixed on the stain in the carpet.

Karl looked quizzically from one to the other. "Yes?" he asked.

Armand looked hard at Amanda, but said nothing, allowing the moment to drag on as Karl continued to look from one to the other.

Amanda finally sat up and faced Karl. "It's like this, Karl. Flattered as I am by Paul Ruffin's request that I should be your understudy, I have very severe reservations about being able to do the job. Even with you there, I don't think I'm ready. In any case, you and I know that Armand would be a much better choice for the job, even if Paul Ruffin doesn't." She paused and took a big breath. "I've been approached to take over the directorship of the Crowley research laboratories. It's a much smaller research lab as you know, but Armand thinks I should accept the offer. I think I can do the Crowley job without too much trouble. That's what's happening." She sat back in her chair and resumed staring at the stain on the carpet.

Karl nodded his head understandingly. "Crowley are a small but very respectable company, Amanda. In your position, I would also have to consider their offer very seriously. I think if the terms and conditions of employment are right, you should accept the offer. But you know I've given you a score of five on the criticality scale, which means you'll have to convince Paul to let you go with all your severance pay intact. He won't like doing that. You see, he's offered me a golden parachute which I cannot refuse. I will be gone by the end of the month, maybe sooner. He's hoping to attract a woman from H & H to replace me. He was planning for you to be in an acting position until she takes over, which may not be for some months. In any case, he's not completely sure that the woman in question wants to come into this 'nest of vipers', as she calls us. She has apparently met a few of us, especially you, Armand, at different conferences and she's uncomfortable about taking the job. She's told Paul she would have to make many changes, which doesn't look good for you, Armand. It may not even be good for you, Amanda. Which is why I think you should accept the job with Crowley, whatever Paul says to you."

Karl stood and went to the window where he stayed looking

out for some moments. He shrugged and, without turning around, said quietly. "So, Armand, the story is unfolding as you predicted. You said I would go, you said the brightest and the best would be pirated away, and the remainder would be hanging on to their jobs by their teeth. This is all very distressing for me, but that's what happens with new bosses. I want to say it's their prerogative, but we all know it stinks."

There was complete silence as each absorbed the implications of the new developments. Amanda continued looking at the stain in the carpet, Armand had also turned round and was looking out of the window at the vista of buildings that together formed a significant proportion of the administrative and productive capacity of AgriBus.

Karl hefted his large body around and motioned to Amanda. "Let's see if Paul is available, that is if you agree you should go to Crowley's. He might just be able to convince you to stay, you never know. But, as you say, it's a great opportunity. You'll be in charge there, which makes a very big difference. Let's go." He went through the door and she followed him out without a word, leaving Armand continuing to look out of the window, his shoulders hunched, his lips pursed in a half-smile as he explored the various options available to him.

Chapter 12

3.00 p.m., Friday, 17 January

Paul Ruffin called the meeting to order. "As you will have observed, there are a couple of new faces in this meeting and a number of faces that are absent. Dr Armand Hernier has joined us as acting head of the Research Department. Dr Karl Helmreich has agreed to take early retirement and thought he should allow Armand an 'unfettered approach to the position', I quote. He will be missed, but I am confident that Armand will do an excellent job as acting head. In addition, you will see that Dr Amanda Fowler is missing from today's meeting. She has accepted an offer from Crowley Pharmaceutical to be their director of research and has also made this her final day with us. We're having a farewell luncheon for both of them this Sunday, to which you and your wives, partners, whatever, are invited. I know this is very short notice, but these farewells happen quickly when they do happen. Isabel will distribute details of the luncheon at the end of our meeting. Incidentally, if some of you can't attend because you've already made other arrangements for the weekend, this will be perfectly understandable. Let Isabel know if you can't make it, for catering purposes. Otherwise, I look forward to seeing you there."

Paul waited as the group around the boardroom table shifted in their seats, pretending they knew nothing about these events. But everyone knew what had taken place in Research. The department was about to come under the direction of a woman who had been enticed from H & H, a woman who had been heard to say very loudly to anyone who cared to listen that she intended to make radical changes in the composition of the personnel and its focus, apparently with Paul Ruffin's blessing. Her reputation as a ruthless and uncompromising taskmaster had preceded her. Heads would roll, including, it was expected, that of the ever-popular Armand Hernier. If that occurred, there was general agreement that mass resignations would follow. A few resignations had already occurred in the department, predictably the brightest and the best, those who saw events in the division as an opportunity to change direction as their loyalties dissolved.

Paul raised his eyes from the notes in front of him. "Having said these things about Doctors Helmreich and Fowler, let me emphasize that I had nothing to do with their resignations. In fact, Amanda Fowler will be sorely missed. And so will the trickle of others who are having little difficulty finding other employment. Armand," Paul turned to look directly at him, "I want you to know I see it as your primary function to do everything you can to stop this haemorrhaging, especially the fives and fours on your personnel list. Furthermore, there is a rumour going around that Helmreich's replacement will make a clean sweep of all key people in the department. That's not true, however much the tendency is for new senior executives to want to surround themselves with their own team, individuals they have worked with and whom they can trust."

Brian Curtis raised his hand. "Is there some inconsistency in what you've just said? My understanding is that Karl Helmreich was given a golden handshake, or have I got it wrong?"

Paul smiled his warm smile. "On the surface, your reasoning is fine, Brian. But there were a number of mitigating circumstances." He sat back in his chair and looked round the table, very conscious of the riveting looks of his key people. "I want you to understand that it's not my practice to justify my decisions on request. However, I propose to make this an exception. I pulled the three most senior people in the Research Department into my office when Amanda resigned. These were Karl, Amanda and Armand. It was evident that Karl, on his own admission, was having great difficulty coping with the administrative demands of his job in the way that I wanted these functions carried out. Bear in mind that I'm not looking simply for a scientist as head of the Research Department, or any specialist in any department for that matter. At that level, I'm almost as much interested in these senior executives being competent administrators, maybe even more so, than scientists or specialists in their field. The last two weeks has illustrated to all of us at our meetings that not only was Karl disinterested in the administrative side of the job, but also he disliked it intensely. It transpires that he did little administrative work under AgriBus direction. My predecessor, Norman Coles, took care of almost all those requirements. This is not the way I manage, as you will have gathered. As an aside, I might argue that it was perhaps his inability to deal with these administrative requirements, and his attempt to push these things onto Amanda Fowler, that caused her to accept the Crowley Laboratories job offer. Be that as it may, we made him an offer to take early retirement, and he accepted it."

"But you already had someone lined up for Karl's job, or are the reports incorrect?" Brian persisted. "Surely that would have had some impact on your decision."

"I never cease to be amazed at the level of information which finds its way into an organization. As a matter of fact, Brian, I had *three* other people as possible backups for the position, all competent scientists: one from H & H, the other two from outside companies. You already know who the H & H person is: Dr Carla Nielson. I believe she will do a good job in Research. Amanda would have complemented her rather well, or so it seemed to me."

"Why not Armand Hernier now that both Karl and Amanda are out of the picture?" continued Brian relentlessly.

Armand leaned forward and interjected quickly. "Brian, this is not open for discussion, *mon ami* . . ."

"That's all right, Armand," Paul interrupted him amiably. "I think everyone must be asking themselves the same question. The sooner we put that behind us, the better." He turned to Brian. "Because Armand informed me, in no uncertain terms, and as only he can inform anyone, that he was not remotely interested in taking the job. The difference financially would be marginal after all his years of service in AgriBus, and the administrative work would be considerable. In any case, his preference is to remain a senior scientist in the department and that's where his very real strengths lie. He's in an acting position because I asked him, as a personal favour, to do the job until Carla Nielson has had a chance to settle in. I also can't imagine who would be a better inductor into the Research Department than Armand. Then she can pick whomever she decides as her deputy, including Armand, if that's the way they both want it."

Paul waited the statutory ten seconds, looking steadily at Brian and then round the rest of the group at the table. "I hope this ends discussion on the issue. And please, all of you, try and make sure the correct message gets around. Nothing destroys morale more effectively than wild rumours which have no basis in fact. That is not to say that such talk doesn't sometimes have an element of truth about it, but it can only be counterproductive, when, as is more often the case, it is well wide of the mark, and also incredibly wasteful of everyone's energies. Hearsay about people coming and going is a highly negative process. Now, let's get on with other business."

He looked carefully at a list in front of him. "In addition to changes at the top of the Research Department, you will see that Dale Cummings is not with us today. With many regrets, Dale resigned yesterday morning without notice and has also vacated his office. It was apparently as much a surprise to Colin as it was to me. The strange thing is that he spent a considerable amount of time developing the criticality scale for everyone in the Division and both Colin and I were delighted with his enthusiasm and effectiveness." Paul shook his head in confusion and shrugged. "That's the way things happen sometimes. Do you want to add anything to that, Colin?"

"As a matter of fact, Paul, I do. I've lost half a dozen good people in the last two weeks, ever since the takeover was officially announced." Colin Marks had that hangdog look which only he could put on when he was unhappy about something. "I don't know why people are deserting so quickly. After all, nothing has changed in the Marketing Department. I mean, it isn't as if Paul fired me and replaced me with some ogre. I'm still here and everybody in Marketing is still in place, working away. Maybe it's the nature of marketing and sales people. I don't know, but it's hurting like hell. I've given exit interviews to every one of these six people, especially Dale. I'm talking about some of our best people, middle managers and supervisors, top performers. The most common answer I receive is that 'It's time for a change', which is absolute nonsense. I could use much stronger language, but I'd better not."

Almost without drawing breath, he continued. "I know takeovers have a nasty reputation. The new bosses come in, rip the place apart, fire people left, right and centre, that sort of thing. It seems to me they could have at least come and talked to me. Instead, they up and resign, goodbye, and they've emptied their desks, taken their pictures off the walls and gone. They don't ask for anything, except their entitlements under the law, and that's it. And they're always the best people too, probably because they're the ones who can find another job easily. Or maybe they already had a job waiting for them in the wings, and all it needed was one phone call and the response, 'When can you start?' type of thing. What does hurt, though, is that they wouldn't tell me why they were leaving, and I pressed each of them very hard. I thought we all got on so well, we always levelled with each other . . ."

Colin Marks took a deep breath and looked around the table,

his eyes finally coming to rest on Paul. "I'm sorry, Paul, I didn't mean to let go like this. But it hurts, you know. I'd treated a couple of these young fellows like they were my own kids. Anyway, I don't know whether my department is unique in this or whether any of you have been experiencing the same problem?"

There was a twenty-second silence as people around the table looked at each other, wondering who would be first to respond to that sensitive question. After all, everyone knew it had as much to do with Colin Marks's own personality as it did with the takeover. "Brian and I have lost a couple of senior technicians and one scientist, but nothing like your experience, Colin," Julian Horne volunteered hesitantly. "In each of the three cases, they saw the two of us together, explained why they were resigning and where they were going, asked for a reference, and took off, going to similar jobs with much bigger salaries. All had been approached at some point recently and they decided it was as good a time as any to leave. But it was all friendly and above board. What was your interpretation of the happenings in our department, Brian?"

"About the same. I think it would probably have happened whether there had been a takeover or not, though not as quickly, perhaps, but who knows. Let me also add that a significant number of Development people have come to either Julian or me to find out what was likely to happen in the short and medium terms, and to ask whether they should begin reviewing their CVs and making phone calls. In every case, we've told them the same thing: if they're doing their jobs properly, they've nothing to worry about, since H & H is not in the business of throwing good people away. I want to add a rider to that: all the people who came to talk to us were people I would want to keep – all fives, fours and a few threes. The ones and twos, and most of the threes, are keeping their heads down, or looking outside and hoping to find a more secure job before the axe comes down here. Not that they know about the criticality scores, which, may I add, Paul, I personally have found to be a highly salutary exercise. It certainly focuses the mind on what matters at the workface."

Paul nodded approvingly. "I'm glad you found the criticality exercise worthwhile. I've always found it very important to do once every six months or so. I've developed my own set of criteria and weights – not that they're that different to the system Dale, John, Isabel and a few others produced for their department and which was adopted by the division. As you say, the analysis focuses your mind on where the weaknesses are in your team. And then – if you're honest with yourself as a manager – you have to ask yourself whether there is anything *you* should have done to improve the performance of the ones and twos. In other words, whether they could possibly be in their current position because you neglected them, or as a result of some other poor managerial input. In any event, it appears that your experience, Julian and Brian, in Development, is different from Colin's in Marketing. Maybe there is something different about scientists and marketing and sales people. It's certainly something we should explore more fully in due course. How about you, Armand? What happened in the Research Department?"

Armand shifted his bulk in the chair and rearranged the papers in front of him, selecting one sheet which he placed carefully on top of the pile. "Let me commence with Amanda. She came to see me about two things. First, she was worried about all the administration work that Karl was giving her, and in particular, the criticality business. She felt she was playing God and she did not like that at all. And second, she told me about the offer from Crowley Laboratories. She did not know what to do about it. I told her the offer was a wonderful opportunity and she must not let it slip by her. I also told her that in the new job, she would have to make decisions about people, indeed as she and Karl were now being asked to make. It came with the territory."

Paul looked quizzically at Armand and demanded, "So you encouraged her to leave H & H?"

Armand returned Paul's look without flinching. "Yes, I did. And so did Karl who came looking for her while she was in my office. I would have advised her to take the job whether we were in a takeover situation or not. And so would you, Paul, if you were in my position."

Paul put on his warm and conciliatory smile "Yes, I would, to be honest. But I might also have tried to keep her in H & H. For someone with Amanda's qualities and strengths, I would have pulled out all the stops to find an equally challenging position in the larger corporation. But then, Armand, you and Karl do not have access to the bigger picture."

Brian raised his hand again. "Why then didn't you pull out all the stops and try to hang on to her when she came in to resign?"

"Another good question, Brian. I had to make my decision as I saw the facts there and then. First, I think she had made up her mind, and secondly it would have taken some time for me to sort out an equivalent or better job for her somewhere in H & H and put a firm offer to her. Third, she may well not have been able to hold the Crowley offer open while all this was going on. It would all have been too rushed, and too risky both for her and for us. So I let her go, with, I have to stress, great regret. We try to hang on to the good ones, especially the women. I don't have to tell any of you about the pressures upon us to find female professionals who are likely to make executive ranks. I think Amanda is one of that breed. Anyway, Brian, that's what happened. And please keep asking these kinds of questions. I know you're not deliberately playing 'devil's advocate', but such exchanges are important in removing any lingering doubts any of you may have about my performance. Now, let's move on. Back to you, Armand. What other people damage is there to report?"

"Before we go on, Paul, what did you mean just now about your performance?" Brian asked.

"Hey! I have to perform in your eyes as much as you have to in mine. No, let me qualify that. I believe it's far more important for me to perform as your boss than it is for you to perform as my subordinates. If you don't think I'm making the grade, I have far greater problems than if you aren't making it. Does anybody have trouble with that reply? Let me elaborate. All of you, in this room, are bosses in your own right. In fact, it's you who are in effect running this operation. If you can't take direction from me – not that I'm trying to present myself as some role model – then you will have difficulty convincing your own subordinates that the way you do things is consistent with our corporate philosophy. You've all had access to the H & H *vision statements*. The very first statement deals with the way we manage our people, our management style. We can't say one thing and then do another, not if these *vision statements* have any meaning at all – and let me assure you, they do have considerable meaning to us at H & H. If I can use a somewhat melodramatic expression, these *vision statements* are what drives us and makes us a successful corporation. Any questions?"

Paul waited again the statutory ten seconds, looking around the table. There were smiles on the faces of some, good smiles, and then there were serious looks on the faces of others, concerned faces that were attempting to assess their own performance as managers. Paul winked at Brian, conveying a "well done" non-verbal message. Brian responded by shrugging, intimating he was happy that his probing questions were providing Paul with the platform from which he could get some management-related thoughts across without having to make it all sound official, maybe even officious.

"Now, Armand, back to you once again."

"Yes, *mes amis*, we have lost about the same number as you, Colin, in Research. And, yes, they were almost all four or better. I did not give them an exit interview because I think it does not serve any useful purpose. If they do not come to you and talk it over with you, like Amanda Fowler, then it is because they do not care to tell you anything which will make you feel better. They have made up their minds, they like where they are going better than being here, usually because the money is much better, and they do not want to be seen to be, what do you say, haggling. They do not want to let you know by how much you have been underpaying them."

Brian interjected once again. "Do you agree with that, Paul?" he asked. "I was always given to understand exit interviews are very important."

"I think they're important," Paul agreed. "How successful they are is a function of the confidence and trust a superior and a subordinate have in each other. Often, of course, exit interviews are conducted by Human Resource counsellors skilled in interpreting responses of employees who have resigned. However, let's not get bogged down with such issues at the moment. What we need to do is stop the haemorrhaging of the brightest and the best, to use your expression, Brian. Any ideas?" and Paul looked round the table at the other seven people present.

"I think people are insecure," Armand immediately responded. "When that happens, they do strange things, like apply for other jobs. We must therefore reassure them that their jobs are secure and that they have no necessity to look at the newspaper vacancies or phone their friends in other companies. Indeed, the brightest and the best have little trouble finding other jobs once the word is out. We need much greater communication."

"I agree completely, Armand," Brian added. "We communicate at our level very well indeed. But how many of us have regular meetings like this with our own immediate subordinates? Answer, we don't. What are your feelings, Julian?" Brian asked his Development Department manager.

Julian Horne hesitated for a moment as he saw himself being manoeuvred into a situation he did not welcome. He had consistently opted for a one-to-one way of managing. He rarely had group meetings despite the urgings of some of his key people, like Brian, who liked the contributions his peers and subordinates invariably brought to the table. "There are other ways of communicating with people in an organization. I think the written word, memos, newsletters, that sort of thing, is more effective than taking up everyone's time in meetings that drag on interminably, as you know, Brian."

Isabel Esporanta, who had never yet spoken unsolicited at these meetings, being largely concerned with taking notes of the proceedings, surprised everyone by affirming, in a quiet voice, "I think there is room for both. I think Paul needs to get round a lot more than he has done, to meet different groups of people at all levels of the division and to talk to them about what's happening. They want to know how H & H works, and how corporate policies might affect them, and they want it direct from the horse's mouth, so to speak. And he also needs to draft memos and newsletters which go out to the whole workforce and tell them what's happening everywhere." Addressing Paul directly, she continued, in her quiet voice, "John and I are constantly moving around all departments, trying to understand what's happening from a systems perspective. We find that most people are hungry for information and spend a great deal of time trying to get us to tell them about H & H, information that I think you, Paul, should be telling them." She resumed her habitual silence, continuing to make notes on her pad as if nothing had happened.

Paul had looked on with an amused smile during that unexpected commentary from Isabel. "John Trury, do you agree with Isabel? I don't of course mean to imply that I don't agree with Isabel. I just want your input as well."

"She's spot on, boss," John Trury replied. "I couldn't have put it better if I'd taken a week to prepare a statement on the matter. Everyone wants to know much more about everything and they want it direct from you. Better still, they would prefer it from the highest sources in H & H. I think there is room for another meeting in a marquee, with the chairman, the president, and as many board members as possible, coming in and talking to them about the future. But they certainly want to see you moving around much more than you've been doing, Paul."

Paul sat back in his chair and looked thoughtfully at the group. He stood up and took a turn across the room. "Makes you sit up and listen when you realize you're letting the side down," he mused, then he faced the group once more. "Let me say that this has been a truly important revelation, and I propose to act on it immediately. I wonder if the best way to tackle the problem initially is to seek the advice of a committee, a special communications committee, who can tell me how to set up a schedule of meetings over the next weeks, even months. And let's not forget the written word. What do you think, people?" He resumed his chair.

As if on cue, John Trury continued, "I think that's an excellent suggestion. Isabel and I should be on that committee. Not that we don't have enough to do, but we do move around the whole of the division and people talk to us. We would bring some important information into such a committee. I also think Colin Marks, or one of his PR people, should help us draft memos, newsletters, and so forth. And then I think either Dr Hernier or Dr Curtis should sit on that committee because they have a long-term understanding, or feeling, if you like, about the division. For what they're worth, Paul, these are my suggestions." John subsided back in his chair.

"And they're excellent suggestions, John. Any comments from anyone else?" Paul waited a few seconds. "Colin, I won't ask you to sit on this committee. You have too much to do. I want you to nominate someone from your department who can help us draft some good PR copy for the workforce. I also think, Armand, that you too have your hands full enough for the moment, but I agree that Brian should join. That's not to say you don't have enough to do, Brian, but I would welcome your input because I know what you can do from the old days. How does that sound, people?"

There was a general murmur of approval. "In which case, I want to meet with the duly constituted Communications Committee on Monday afternoon at 4 p.m. in this boardroom. Colin, select a PR specialist and tell him or her to join us then. Now, people, let's get on with other matters on our agenda."

Brian raised his hand once more. "Before we move on, and

while we're still on absent faces, have you given some thought to the matter of including Tony Johns on this committee?"

"Yes, I have," Paul replied quickly. "I don't think it would be appropriate to have him on this committee. And I hasten to add that I don't want to go into this matter any further at this point. Now, let's move on."

Chapter 13

2.30 p.m., Sunday, 26 January

"There's no doubt about you, Brian and Gretl, you put on a mighty barbecue," Paul Ruffin informed them, rubbing his stomach. "What do you think, Beebee?" he asked her, leaning closer and refilling her glass from a half-empty bottle of wine standing by her place mat.

"Darling," Britt Berghoff replied, treating him to a wink that only she could endow with such sexual promise, "the Curtises have set a standard we have all tried to reach for years, so it is no surprise you have enjoyed the food. But now comes the best part. We sit here and we drink and we talk and we laugh a lot. Then we go home and sleep for twelve hours," she purposely allowed her voice to drop a decibel or two, "after we make furious love."

"That sounds great, Beebee. I only wish Mary were here too, but then, she doesn't drink very much and she would take great exception to making love in the afternoon."

Britt shook her head sadly. "What a pity, what a shame. If my Ron were here, I think she would change her mind. He would make her think of other things, let me tell you." She turned to Michelle who was sitting opposite her and had been watching this development with increasing concern. "Do you agree, darling? My Ronny, he is something else?"

Michelle didn't hesitate. "I agree completely, *ma chère* Beebee. You tell us he is a great lover, but I think he is also very jealous, don't you think? Anyway," she continued quickly, "I think it is a great shame he had to go on this computer course. You would enjoy meeting him, Paul. He is not only a great motor mechanic, he is also a very intelligent young man."

"Bully for him, Michelle." Paul turned to her, taking his eyes off Britt with obvious difficulty. "You say he is young?" he asked. "How young, Beebee?" His gaze was drawn back to the Berghoff curves.

"My Ron," she answered with a knowing smile, "he is twenty-four and as strong as a young bull."

Paul sat back in his canvas chair and smiled his warmest smile. He was unmistakably enjoying this unexpected flirtation and had hardly taken his eyes off Britt since he had arrived. But then, she was wearing an extremely tight-fitting lime-green cashmere pullover and no bra. In addition, she had on a pair of white trousers which she must have had enormous difficulty zipping up. The total effect was to accentuate every inch of her voluptuous figure. For Paul, looking the complete debonair senior executive, in an open-necked canary-yellow shirt underneath a brown tartan pullover and pale blue slacks, had given her one look on arrival and hardly left her side thereafter. To the Curtises and the Herniers, the chemistry which flowed so evidently between their two companions spelt trouble. However, as Armand had firmly but quietly reminded the other three, they were dealing here with two grown-ups who had obviously been around and should know what they were doing. So the four of them proceeded to ignore as far as they could the not-too-covert signals which continuously passed between Britt and Paul.

Gretl Curtis looked meaningfully at Michelle Hernier. "Time for coffee." They both stood. "Brian, will you look after the port? Beebee, would you give us a hand?" and the two wives quickly made their exit from the sundeck in the direction of the kitchen. Britt paused long enough to give Paul a little nudge and a smile, and slowly stood and followed Gretl and Michelle, the three men watching her every sensuous movement as she disappeared into the house.

Paul shook his head as if to clear his thoughts. "Wow, as they say in Hollywood. That is some woman. And she topped her class in toxicology? Wow," he repeated.

"We know, Paul," Brian assured him. "What you see in her labcoat and what you see at other times are at opposite ends of the spectrum. We haven't stopped ogling her since she joined AgriBus some eleven years ago. She was a lot thinner then, but the potential was there and it's blossomed beyond even our lecherous imaginations ever since." He looked meaningfully at Armand. "Your turn to rave, Armand."

"Oh! *mon cher* Brian. It does me no good to think about such matters. Two of us with such magnificent proportions would require extraordinary contortions, which would be quite exhausting. But, on occasion, Paul, when I do think about our dear Beebee . . . oo là là!" and he gestured emphatically in true Gallic fashion.

Brian stood. "Time for a port," and he also went into the house, leaving Armand and Paul to enjoy the languor of the afternoon in silence.

Paul looked across to Armand, studying him carefully. "What made you leave France, Armand, and what made you stay on here?" he asked quietly, taking advantage of the relaxed atmosphere, good food, and excellent wine. "Circumstances like that intrigue me. I hope you don't mind my asking." His eyes assumed their veiled businesslike intensity.

Armand returned Paul's intense look, his fat jowls bobbing up and down in quiet mirth. There was little doubt Armand understood Paul well enough to know that he was never very far from business, whatever the distractions. "It is not difficult to understand, *mon ami*," he replied. "You come for a consultancy, you stay a little longer than planned because they keep asking you so nicely to stay, and then, suddenly, you have been here twelve years. Your children have grown up, your wife has made a whole new group of friends, and you don't dislike your job too much. Life has taken over, *et voilà, c'est l'histoire de ma vie*, as some stupid poet once said, I cannot remember who."

Paul nodded quietly to himself. "I'd like to believe that's all there is to it. But I know there's much more to it than that. You have, by all accounts, a prodigious capacity for hard work and, more importantly, significant work. You should be managing a large group of scientists and producing spectacular results. Instead, I find you buried in a human ethicals backwater like AgriBus, fiddling with peripheral development work, instead of pure research."

"Perhaps, *mon ami*, perhaps. I do not have to tell you, we continue to do what we do, however trivial others may find it, for a variety of reasons. Perhaps one of them is that I have no ambition. Perhaps another is that I do not want to make my employer rich. A third possibility is that your diagnosis of me is completely wrong, that I am not such a hard worker and can produce little of significance after all because I am really quite stupid. So, if that is true, you should fire me, especially since I am not a hot favourite with my future boss, Dr Carla Nielson. Maybe that is what I have been waiting for: to be uncovered and to be fired. Then I would go back to France and you would have your answer."

"That's all too easy, Armand. I'm not going to fire you. But I am going to put a red hot poker under your behind, if only because I think you are one heck of a good scientist and Carla Nielson is going to need you very badly so I can make my employer rich and you can make me famous."

Armand's jowls continued to bob up and down as he laughed quietly to himself. "I can see we are going to have a lot of fun, you, your Carla Nielson, and me. I think you will find my *derrière* has been assailed with many hot pokers, but with little success."

Brian returned with the three girls in time to hear that remark. "What's all this about hot pokers under your behind, Armand?

Don't tell me Paul is threatening to do what Karl Helmreich, Norman Coles and a dozen others before them have failed to do all your life. I should have warned you, Paul, nothing moves our beloved Armand unless he wants to move. And it has nothing to do with his mass. Am I right, Michelle, or am I right?" Brian placed a tray holding the port decanter and half a dozen port glasses on the outdoor wooden table and proceeded to pour.

"That is true, Paul," she replied, putting down a platter with a large camembert, dry biscuits and grapes. "But it is also true that, if you can get him moving, it is almost impossible to bring him to a standstill. He will not stop until he has finished whatever it is he is doing. He is not easy to manage, let me tell you, Paul. I have tried to give him away to Beebee here, and to other German, even French ladies, but no one wants to take him off my hands. I am stuck with him, and I love him just the way he is," she said, leaning over and giving Armand a big kiss.

"Lucky man, Armand. No one's ever said that to me," Paul responded, assuming once again his warm smile.

"Maybe that is because you have never given them a chance, darling. You move too quickly for most women. But not for me. I will catch you, hold you down, and never let you go," Britt exclaimed as she moved over Paul, placing his head in a half-lock and rubbing her ample breasts against the back of his head.

Paul raised his hands above his head in surrender. "Beebee, I give up. You have me forever. You can do whatever you like, as long as you promise not to stop. I love it."

As this unashamed exhibition of sexual attraction was being acted out, the door chime rang, immediately followed by a voice from the direction of the front entrance. "Where is everyone?" To the immense relief of Gretl and Michelle, Tony and Gloria Johns appeared on the sundeck, immediately taking in the view of the voluptuous senior scientist from the Development Department with a headlock on the hitherto incorruptible general manager of the newly acquired Human Ethicals Division of H & H.

The appearance of these two newcomers did nothing to deter the irrepressible Britt Berghoff, but it had quite the opposite effect on Paul Ruffin, who seized Britt's arms and dragged them none too gently from around his head. Pushing her away, he immediately stood up and straightened his shirt and pullover.

"A moment of joyous abandon," he announced, the warm smile appearing on his face as if by magic. He took the necessary five paces to Tony Johns and held out his hand. "Good to see you, Tony," he said. "We were just playing, as you will have gathered." He turned to Gloria who was standing perfectly still, obviously bewildered by the scene and the response. "You must be Tony's wife, Gloria. I'm so glad to meet you at last." He took her hand in his and held it for just a moment too long, and then returned to Britt. "All good things must come to an end, Beebee," he said quietly. "My apologies but, as you see, we had better behave ourselves from now on, don't you think?" And he sat her down, patted her on the shoulder and made way for Gloria to take the seat next to her.

"As a matter of fact," he continued, looking at Brian and Gretl, "I ought to be getting along. I'll pass on the coffee and port, Brian. Duty calls, if you know what I mean, old friend." He circled the table quickly, patted Armand on the shoulder, winked at Michelle, waved at the Johns who had sat down at the table and, accompanied by a bewildered Brian and Gretl, went into the house. The others heard him make his final goodbyes to the Curtises, and, a moment later, his Jaguar started up and moved quietly away down the street.

Brian and Gretl returned to the sundeck and busied themselves pouring coffee and port. For two or three minutes, not a word was said.

As Brian handed her a port, Gloria Johns remarked tartly, "We Johnses seem to have a dampening effect on people these days. I told you we should have gone home, Tony."

Michelle replaced her coffee on the table. "I am glad you didn't, Gloria. I am not sure what would have happened if you had not arrived when you did." She glared across at Britt.

"Oh, well, madam purity," Britt spat forward, her prominent chin thrust out, ready for battle. "Just because he did not pay any attention to you . . ."

"Hey, you two," Gretl quickly interrupted. "Michelle, I love you dearly, but Beebee didn't deserve that comment. And Beebee, relax. As far as the rest of us are concerned, both you and Paul are old enough to know how to conduct yourselves with friends. I'm just sorry it had to happen as you two arrived, Gloria, but somehow your appearance reminded Paul he should behave himself. Which in some ways was a pity. I would have liked to know how far you would have gone, you gorgeous hussy," she said with a mischievous grin, turning to Britt.

"Not you too, Gretl," Britt replied. "I was having a bit of fun, that is all. Anyhow, I think I would have enjoyed a tumble with our chief."

"Not today, Josephine," Brian observed with a huge smirk on his face. "Nonetheless, why *did* he break off with Beebee, I wonder, just when things were getting interesting? I never knew him previously to act this way. At college he was always a great one for the ladies, as I recall, and he certainly never gave up quite that easily."

"Because he suddenly realized that he was being very stupid," Armand commented. "My mother, God rest her soul, used to say that when you work in the East, you do your courting in the West. I have always followed that advice – not that Michelle would ever let me get away with anything like this."

"*Mon petit chou*," she responded with an edge to her voice, "if that is the way you want to go, please do so. Just leave the keys to the house and the cars with me on your way out."

It was Brian's turn to intercede. "Hey, you two, knock it off. Something happened here this afternoon which had nothing to do with any of us. It was up to Paul to decide in which direction he wanted to run. He chose to run out. Possibly it was because he suddenly realized that he was carrying on rather foolishly – which . . ." he turned to Britt, ". . . he was, whatever you, my darling Beebee, may have thought would be fun. So, let's drink our coffee and port, tuck into that delicious cheese and biscuits, and enjoy this wonderful and quite unseasonable weather we are having. Welcome, Gloria and Tony, I'm sorry you had to miss the barbecue but it's great you were able to join us after all." And he raised his glass to the others, waited until they had all somewhat reluctantly picked up their glasses, and drank his port down in one gulp.

It was going to be one of these occasions, he decided, when everyone was determined to be uptight. After all, Tony still didn't know whether he would have a job for much longer and he was giving Gloria a hard time as a result. Armand wasn't looking forward to working with Carla Nielson, despite Paul's assurances that she would welcome his help. And Michelle wasn't making life any easier for him by being very touchy about his unabashed admiration for Britt, particularly when she displayed her considerable allure in an intimate setting such as this barbecue. As for Beebee, it had been a while since she had been anywhere without her Ron, and the appearance of a good-looking and suave lone male on the scene had apparently been too tempting. Well, thank heavens he and Gretl still seemed to be functioning normally. The coming weeks would be decision time for everyone in the HE Division, especially everyone around the table, including himself. He poured himself another port and passed the decanter along. He wasn't about to start worrying about these imponderables, certainly not on such a glorious afternoon. There was nothing he could do to influence the way the drama was unfolding. He again gulped down his glass of port, glanced sheepishly at Gretl who was looking at him inquiringly, and settled back in his chair to enjoy the last of the winter sun.

Part IV

Changes everywhere

Chapter 14

3.00 p.m., Friday, 1 February

On the stroke of three Paul entered the boardroom and sat down. He glanced briefly around the table. Without uttering a word, he took a number of copies of a sheet from a folder and passed these around. He waited till everyone had taken a good look at the contents of that document and then informed them in a quiet, matter-of-fact tone, "These are the people I've been asked by Head Office to retire without delay, notwithstanding their criticality scores. They have five things in common: they've been with AgriBus for over twenty years, mostly on the agricultural side; they transferred to the HE Division within the last seven years; they've been in the same positions for five or more years and there is no indication they're likely to be promoted any further; they're in salary ranges well above the average for the positions they hold; and finally, they're over fifty years of age." He waited as pens ran down the list and marks were made against names. "Questions?" he asked, his voice casual, his body relaxed.

There was suddenly a tenseness in the boardroom that Brian had never felt as distinctly before. The four line managers sat in stunned silence for another minute, while Isabel Esporanta and John Trury, sitting on either side of Paul as usual, lowered their heads in expectation of the storm. The bloodbath was about to begin and the reduction in the workforce by process of attrition had come to an end. It wasn't so much that it was unexpected. What hurt were the choices of people who were being forcibly retired, a good number close friends and associates of members of that senior executive group, and all with high scores of five and four. It made the criticality exercise, on which they had placed so much reliance as a determinant of who stayed and who went, a total sham.

"Did you ask for questions? You bet, Paul," Colin Marks spoke up. "You've just decimated my managerial people. If they all go, I won't be able to operate the Marketing Department."

"That appears to be the intention of head office, Colin. They've decided to run your Marketing Department down over some months and transfer what's left to a new head office marketing division dealing exclusively with prescription drugs. I have to admit that this is as much a surprise to me as it is to you. Anyway, that's the way it is."

"And the promises made at the time of the takeover, what has happened to them?" Armand asked Paul, leaning forward and fixing him with an unwavering stare, his face tight with suppressed anger.

"More importantly, where are these people going to find jobs at their ages? Hell, Paul, many of them are close to retirement," Brian added, looking down at the list before him.

Paul nodded and stood, as he did when he had to deal with a contentious issue for which he had no immediate answer. He walked back and forth across the width of the boardroom twice, the silence palpable. Without pausing in his stride, his head down, speaking to no one in particular, he said, "Let me see if I can explain what I believe is going on at the highest levels of the corporation. First of all, some facts. The pharmaceutical industry is divided more or less into two areas: prescription drugs and over-the-counter products, OTC as it's more commonly called. OTC products run from cold and headache formulations to cosmetics and shampoos. Prescription drugs are exactly what that expression intimates: they're drugs which can only be obtained with a doctor's prescription from a qualified pharmacist."

Without pausing, he continued. "The AgriBus HE Division was and is exclusively in the prescription drug business. H & H, on the other hand, is substantially in the OTC area, which accounts for over 70 per cent of its revenue. It has done very nicely over the years out of OTC and is generally regarded as an industry leader. Its sophisticated packaging and advertising, its diversified penetration of the retail trade, especially the large chain stores, is undoubtedly its great strength. However, in spite of its size, both domestically and internationally, there has been a steady erosion of its market share, largely because it is now competing with the backyarder, the small manufacturer, and also with the large chemical companies, which have moved strongly into the mainstream of its OTC product range. The bottom line is that if H & H is to continue to grow and prosper, it must do so in prescription drugs."

There was a noticeable shifting of bottoms on seats and feet on the carpet as he came to a standstill behind his chair and looked around the table. He had told them nothing they didn't already know and they were impatiently waiting for something, anything, which would justify the dismantling of the Marketing Department and other support functions, maybe even the whole division.

He continued, his voice even, the tone modulated, the explanation taking on a detachment which discouraged interruptions and questions. "Whereas the largest proportion of expense in OTC is in marketing, in the broadest sense of that word, when it comes to prescription drugs, by far the greatest expense is in research and development. The big breakthrough, like the discovery of penicillin, prednisone, Tagamet, levodopa, even the discovery of a more effective diuretic or a more potent anti-inflammatory for rheumatoid arthritis, that's what human ethical drug companies live for. And this breakthrough has eluded H & H . . .", he paused for effect, "as well as the AgriBus HE Division."

He stopped pacing the floor and singled out Armand, returning his direct stare. "If H & H as a pharmaceutical company hasn't gone under, it's because of OTC. If the HE Division of AgriBus was sold off, it's because agricultural products refused to continue paying the cost. Yes, there's a lot of glamour in discovering something new, something which attenuates suffering a little, even saves human lives. But the associated costs are enormous."

Once again he stopped speaking, noticing the diminishing impatience with his line of explanation as they began to understand where he was taking them. He held up his hand, a signal to the group he hadn't finished. "To make money in prescription drugs," he continued, "you have to spend money, buckets of it, without any assurance of a return. We're talking about employing clinical pharmacologists, physiologists, chemists, biologists, toxicologists, pathologists, veterinarians, even statisticians, and heaven knows how many other specialists, all in great demand by the pharmaceutical companies, and all in high salary brackets. Then there are the research facilities, not wood or aluminium, but nothing less than stainless steel. Why stainless steel? Because anything less can harbour micro-organisms, germs, any of which can contaminate weeks, months, even years of research. Then the animals, hundreds, thousands of them: rats, mice, pigs, dogs, cats, monkeys, all germ-free and born and bred at great expense in captivity for the sole purpose of being used in HE experiments. Then there are tests on human subjects, also very expensive. And to top it all off, you have to contend with the extraordinarily strict requirements of the regulatory authorities."

He sat down heavily in his chair. They were now listening intently. "We are talking about as many as ten years of unwavering commitment to an idea before a drug is approved for use, and an expenditure over that period of as much as two to three hundred million dollars. Then there's the possibility that a drug, in spite of all the safeguards, may have devastating side effects: for example, thalidomide, Oraflex, Bendectine, implants of various kinds. True, not many in the total scheme of things – in fact, only a tiny proportion of the many successful drugs that have transformed medical practice – but these rogue drugs, for want of a better word, have generated litigation which has ruined some highly reputable corporations. The long and the short of the story is that prescription drugs are extraordinarily expensive to discover, and fraught with difficulties and dangers. But we also know how important, in every way, especially financially, a discovery can be. For example, Procardia, Indocin, Orinase, Tagamet, prednisone, and many other drugs that are prescribed by doctors every day because they help cure people and, by the by, make the discoverers wealthy beyond their wildest imaginings."

Julian Horne broke in, his voice unexpectedly sharp and strident, "With respect, Paul, where is this thumbnail sketch of our industry leading to?"

"You want me to spell it out? OK. Unless we get serious about results and we stop thinking about the HE Division as some fancy club for a bunch of highbrow technocrats who think they are owed a living, and a very good one at that, all of us are facing the high jump. And this goes for H & H prescription drug employees as well."

He returned Armand's frozen stare with equal intensity. And then he turned to Julian Horne. "I haven't been told any of this officially, but it doesn't take a genius to work out that head office propose to do whatever it takes to turn the prescription drug operation into a winning proposition. They're doing what successful pharmaceutical companies have been doing for years: they're creating a prescription drug company which they hope will stand on its own and will be able to justify its existence in strict financial terms. The creation of a marketing organization exclusively for prescription drugs is the first step. The next will probably be to bring together technocrats who have similar research interests, give them the support they need and see how quickly they can produce worthwhile results."

"And if we don't, what you say, produce?" Armand asked harshly.

"They'll get rid of us and get people who can. We're all under the gun, gentlemen, and I mean everyone everywhere in H & H. We're just going to have to start earning our keep, that's all there is to it. In addition to those on the list, for the immediate future, which technocrats are kept and which are retired will depend on an analysis of the reports I, and other HE Division heads everywhere in the company, submitted to head office during the second half of last month. For your information, my report was based on the review of activities you prepared for me early last month." Paul leaned forward, his elbows on the table, his fingers interlaced. "What else can we profitably discuss?"

Armand was still on the offensive. "Specifically, how are these people going to be fired?" indicating the sheet in front of him.

"I hope as constructively and sensitively as possible."

"Which means?" Armand persisted.

"To begin with, I propose to do that job myself, Armand. If you want a blow-by-blow description, I would be very happy to describe the process to you."

"I would very much like to hear how H & H fire people," Armand continued as aggressively as ever, leaning back in his chair, his arms crossed on his chest. "After all, *monsieur le directeur*, since a good third of my colleagues in Research are having their lives ruined because they are over fifty years of age, which should include me, please note, except I am forty-nine, it interests me particularly, *non*? In addition, *monsieur le directeur*," his sarcasm permeating every syllable of every word, "I shall be fifty in ten months. Does this mean I will also have to go?"

Paul shrugged and smiled at Armand, indicating in that simple non-verbal gesture his resignation at having to deal with fractious subordinates like Armand. "*Mais oui, monsieur le docteur*," he replied, "I will do my best to explain."

Paul nodded at Isabel Esporanta who distributed another sheet to the four senior managers. Once again, he waited for them to examine that document.

"Each of these people on the list will be asked to come to my office where I will explain the contents of that sheet. At the end of the meeting, they will be escorted to their offices, they will pack their personal effects, they will be taken to their cars and they will drive away, never to return. On the surface, it looks absolutely callous and heartless. In fact, as you can see, the company is making an extraordinary effort to help them adjust to their changed circumstances. I should stress that every possible redundancy entitlement is being applied so that each employee will walk away from our meeting with the full measure of benefits that the law allows. After that, a broad range of services will be available to every person who chooses to use them.

"First, a highly reputable consultancy of outplacement specialists have been contracted to help them manage the period of transition between jobs. I'm talking here about counselling, office and phone facilities, training in job search techniques, anything which will help. The most obvious initial enquiry will be to see whether they can transfer back to AgriBus. It may not be to equivalent positions with the same pay, but there may be one or two acceptable openings.

"Second, where necessary, further essential groundwork for finding a job will be undertaken under the direction of the consultants. The preparation of professional CVs, how to make the most of available job opportunities, the careful drafting of covering letters, training in phone and face-to-face interviews, and so on. In other words, each person will be given individual attention in order to optimize his or her chances of finding a suitable position, or of making the best adjustment for retirement. How am I doing, Doctor Hernier?"

Armand returned Paul's direct look, but said nothing.

"Any other questions, gentlemen?" He waited the usual ten seconds, his eyes going from one to the other.

"In that case, one final comment on that subject. At this precise moment, there is no document in the HE Division as confidential as the list you have before you. If I am to do any kind of a half-decent job as your division general manager in dealing with this highly sensitive redundancy situation, it will be because I want you to say nothing to any of your subordinates." He held up his hand as all four started to speak at the same time. "I know it will be difficult to continue working with these people and pretend their jobs are still secure. But that responsibility goes with your positions in the company. As department managers and my most senior executives, you will appreciate that I don't want to have to face people who have been stewing for a few hours, maybe a day or two, and are primed to make their interview with me any more difficult than it will already be. I shan't ask you to return that sheet. I have to trust you to do the right thing by me, and by your colleagues. Most of all, I have to trust you to let me do my job, disagreeable as it will be for all of us around this table."

He closed the file before him and put it aside. "In any event," he continued abstractly, his mind already on other matters, "I can only reassure you I will go through the interviews as rapidly as I can, being as sensitive and considerate as I can. Now let's move on to other matters . . ."

Chapter 15

1.00 p.m., Tuesday, 19 February

Gloria pushed the piece of feta cheese around the edge of her plate with her fork for the third time, ignoring most of her appetizing Greek salad. She had hardly eaten any of it, while Gretl and Michelle had finished theirs. The three friends had eaten in silence for the last few minutes, lost in their own thoughts.

Unable to watch Gloria's pain any further, Michelle leaned gently over and held her hand. "Darling," she said quietly, "it will not do for you to feel so much. Everything will be all right, nothing is surer."

Gloria was not to be mollified so easily. "Everything will not be all right, Michelle. At his age, where can he find another job? And he still has so much to give. This is what upsets me more than anything else. It isn't as if he hasn't done a good job for AgriBus and would do a good job for Helm & Hathaway. Let me tell you, over the years, he's saved AgriBus again and again from being sued out of existence. I know one might argue that this is what he was being paid to do. But he was prepared to argue against everyone when he felt the company was getting itself into trouble. It didn't make him popular, but he didn't care. He kept putting his point of view until he was satisfied that every eventuality had been covered and that the company could extricate itself from any sticky legal situation. This is what made him different . . ."

Gretl interrupted, her voice sharp and businesslike. "Gloria, I want you to do two things for me right now. First, I want you to finish your salad. You've hardly touched it and you're the salad lover out of the three of us. We've continued coming every third Tuesday in every month to The Salad Bowl for heaven knows how long only because you've always insisted that lunch may as well be healthy and mouth-watering. Second, I want us to talk about something other than H & H and what they're doing to the Human Ethicals Division, Tony included. Let's face it, they've finally started making decisions which are not completely unexpected. In fact, Tony is the one who consistently reminded us that we were overstaffed, over confident and over paid, and one day things would catch up with us. Well, they have, except that no one thought Tony would be one of the casualties – no one, that is, except Tony himself. I agree with Michelle. Tony is a rare mixture of excellent education, skills and experience and I think he'll be snapped up as soon as word gets round that he's available."

"It still seems so unfair, Gretl. He could have been any kind of lawyer when he graduated, earning a good living with a secure future. But he chose the pharmaceutical industry because he wanted to help make it responsible. I think it was partly because his mother became hooked on opium and died miserably in an asylum. What a ridiculous industry it is. I mean, think of it. In 1898, Kelloggs introduced Cornflakes specifically as an anti-constipation food. In the late 1950s, the military were still mixing bromide in tea as an anti-aphrodisiac with the purpose of reducing the sex drives of their soldiers. By the end of the 1960s, drug companies had produced over two-and-a-half thousand different kinds of 'me-too' barbiturates which they were peddling to doctors as cures for every possible human problem, physical and psychological. Not to mention addiction, which is still so common today because drug companies are pushing doctors to prescribe their 'me-too' drugs in increasing frequency and hang the consequences, and because doctors can't go to the trouble of reading Department of Health warnings. The catalogue of stupidity and cupidity is endless, as Tony would put it."

Gloria speared the lump of feta cheese she had been pushing around her plate and chewed on it ferociously. "These are the things Tony has been fighting, not only in AgriBus, but at every conference he's attended. The consequence is that he's known as a troublemaker. That's why he thinks no drug company will employ him. You know what he's doing this morning, Gretl? He's attending a course which is going to make him be a better interviewee, when he knows he will never be interviewed for a job again. He has two telling factors against him: his age and his reputation. I'm worried, Gretl. I'm worried for a man, a good man, who has given the best years of his life to his job and now has nowhere to go, except down."

Once again, Michelle covered Gloria's hand with her own. "*Ma chère*, you are overreacting. It is still very early days. After all, Tony finished at the company only two weeks ago. He is doing very much the right thing making use of the consultants. Armand would do exactly the same thing in his shoes."

Gloria snatched her hand away from Michelle. "But Armand is not in his shoes. What's more, he has probably never had to interview for a job in his life, let alone been fired."

"I think you're being rather unfair, Gloria," Gretl quickly broke in. "Michelle is only trying to be helpful."

"Well, she hasn't been living with Tony for the last two weeks, or she would understand why I can't eat this wretched salad and why I'm angry," Gloria shot back. Then she suddenly realized that she was taking her frustrations out on her friends, which was both unfair and hurtful. She turned to Michelle, who by now was looking thoroughly miserable. "I'm sorry, Michelle, I didn't mean it that way. I'm simply very uptight. It's been very difficult over the last few days. You know how Tony can be."

She put her fork on her plate, making a conscious effort to be calm and affable. Looking from one to the other of her friends, she smiled. "So, what else has been happening in the world?"

Michelle brightened up immediately, her hand reaching out to Gloria once again. "I know it is only February, but I wish we were going back to the beach house again soon. It was so much fun and December is such a long way away . . ."

Chapter 16

8.15 p.m., Friday, 1 March

Britt Berghoff sat on the rotating bar stool watching Ron wash the dinner plates and then dry them. They had agreed, when he first moved into her town house, that since he knew so little about cooking, she would prepare the meals, and he would set the table, clear up and wash the dishes. She liked watching him doing his chores. As with everything else, he did even these simplest of things with an intensity, a concentration, which constantly surprised her. It explained why he had so successfully mastered the most complex computer programming exercises he brought home from his evening classes. She also liked the way the muscles rippled on his arms as he dried the dishes with a gentleness which belied his large, calloused hands. But most of all, she loved his long blond hair which he tied in a ponytail. She remembered the quarrel they had when he wanted to cut his hair short, "in keeping with my girlfriend's station in life", he informed her. Well, she won, telling him she had no such thing as "a station in life". She was the same immigrant girl who put herself through school and then university and she had no pretensions to being anything else.

She thought back to that ridiculous afternoon with Paul Ruffin and how she had almost been unfaithful to her Ronny, saved only by the arrival of Gloria and Tony Johns. But what a startling effect their arrival had had on Paul. One minute he was all over her, ready to spring into bed, the next he had taken off like a scared rabbit, leaving his coffee and port untouched, much to everyone's amazement. The only logical explanation was that he must have already known he was about to fire Tony, and he couldn't handle a social situation where he would have to pretend that nothing had changed in their business relationship. No one had commented on his strange behaviour, but they were evidently relieved he had departed without taking her with him. Well, that would be her last flirtation. She couldn't imagine being with anyone other than her gorgeous, clever, uncomplicated Ronny.

Ron replaced the tea towel on its hook under the sink, wiped down the bench, looked carefully around the kitchen to make sure he had left nothing undone and came around the counter. Without saying a word, he took Britt by the arm and led her into the softly lit living room. They sat side by side on the comfortable three-seater lounge chair, as they almost always did, their hips touching, her back half resting on his chest while he massaged her neck.

"Now tell me what's been going on at work. You don't look too happy tonight," he told her, continuing to massage her neck.

"You know me too well, darling. Some people would say that is not good, but I love it. Yes, just there. A little harder, darling. I feel as if I have one big knot there. Yes, that feels so good. Keep going."

She wriggled appreciatively closer into his chest. "What is happening at work? The place is like a cemetery. Everyone is going around as if there has been one enormous death. Not a single person has not lost a good friend, someone with whom they worked and played, you know what I mean. For me, it is very strange not to have Tony come into my laboratory twice a day and pat me on the bottom. I miss him badly. So do Brian and Armand. They are walking around like, how do you say, ghosts. No, that is not right. Anyway, Brian is very sad and Armand is very angry. I had lunch with them today in the canteen. I think morale is very low everywhere. It seems like everyone is waiting for the next round of firings. It is not good, let me tell you. They pretend they are working, but they are not doing anything productive. They mostly sneak around corners, in the lavatories, in the coffee room, talking about this one and that one and how they are not dealing well with being fired. This one is now having trouble with a girlfriend or boyfriend, or husband or wife, and they are all running around like chickens without their heads looking for jobs. And now, suddenly, the job market is tight. One month ago, if you asked any of them about job prospects, they would tell you they could walk out today and find a better one tomorrow. Well, I don't understand what is going on. Maybe I have been a scientist too long. This will be my twelfth year, Ronny. It has gone so quickly, and now I am thirty-eight."

"Maybe it's time you moved on, Bee," he observed quietly, continuing to knead her shoulders with his strong, gentle, fingers.

"You know, darling, I was thinking the same thing. So I went to Human Resources on Wednesday and had them find out what I would get if I resigned. They had to go to Helm & Hathaway's head office for that. The answer came back this afternoon. If I leave the company now, I get a big payout. H & H have made AgriBus employees a special offer to go. Let me show you, Ronny."

She reached for her handbag on the coffee table in front of her, rummaged around inside for a moment and retrieved an envelope. Without saying a word, she gave him the single sheet of paper on which was a table of dates, headings and numbers, with CONFIDENTIAL written in bold red letters at the top.

Ron studied the document carefully for a moment and gave a low whistle. "This is after tax?" he asked her.

"Yes, darling. I went through the figures with the people in

Human Resources when they phoned to tell me they had the details. If I leave at the end of this month, this is what I get."

"You could set yourself up in your own business with that amount of cash, Bee," he told her, handing the sheet of paper back to her. "You could borrow three times as much again if you had a good business idea. And the government will give you all sorts of tax rebates and allowances if you're a new small business and more if you employ and train some people, and so on." He returned to kneading her shoulders. "I'm joking, Bee. Anyway, it'll all blow over and things will return to normal. Sure, it won't be the same for you without friends like Tony at work. But we'll never stop being close to them, will we? They probably need friendship now even more than before, don't you think?"

He stopped kneading her shoulders and turned her around to face him. "Why don't you phone Gloria now. Let's have them over for your special beef stroganoff tomorrow night, if they're free. We've got all the ingredients and there's tons of everything. I think they'd like a bit of cheering up. If they can come, phone Gretl and Brian, and Michelle and Armand. Let's have a party, and to hell with all these problems. I've got these six bottles of 1989 Penfolds Shiraz I've been saving for a special occasion. What do you say?"

Britt reached out and pulled his face down to hers. "You know, Ronny, darling, I love you. You are a truly wonderful man." She gave him a lingering kiss. "I will do that in just a moment. But first we must have a serious talk."

She sat away from him and placed the sheet with the payout numbers between them in a symbolic gesture. "This", she started, pointing at the paper, "is something I have never thought about. I suppose you do not think of things like this when you are thirty-eight. Ten, fifteen years from now, as I get closer to retirement, I will begin to think about these things, like Tony and Gloria must be doing. Of course, they still have children to educate, that kind of thing, no? I do not. Maybe it is because I am too selfish. I do not know. But this is a good time for me to decide if I really want to remain in a laboratory for the rest of my life, with microscopes, mice, chemicals, testing this and that, mostly walking away from an experiment that has cost many millions, shaking my head as things go kaput."

She stood and walked over to the trolley which they had turned into a bar, poured two large ports and brought them back to the couch. "And then there is the sitting around in meetings, hour after hour, as we look over our research and development programme, trying to make a drug just a little better than the competition so that we can sell a little more. Except that this time, we hope it is not going to hurt anyone. And we wonder if, this time, some unknown side effect might just prove harmful to people so that their families sue the company and make us go out of business."

Ron reached out and took her hand. "Hey, sweetheart, I've never heard you talk like this before. Are you telling me you make drugs that hurt people?"

"We try not to, darling, and we test and test. But there is always a doctor out there who is going to prescribe our drug to a patient, give him too much, or too little, or even diagnose the illness wrongly, and yes, harm, even kill that patient. And it is not always the fault of the doctor. Often it is because the patient thinks if he takes three or four doses at once, it will make him better three or four times more quickly. And then, of course, there is always the patient who reacts badly to our drug, usually because he or she is taking our drug with all sorts of other drugs and they don't mix well. I could tell you some terrible stories, Ronny. And all the time our Tony tries to make us continue testing and, if not, make sure we say things on our promotion material, the stuff we give doctors, and the reports we prepare for different government departments, so that we stay out of trouble if something goes wrong."

"Hey!" Ron exclaimed, shaking his head, "this is some business you're in. I didn't know when I go to see a doctor and he gives me an injection or even a pill, he could, well, like be doing the wrong thing. This is heavy stuff, Bee."

"Before you go too far, darling, only one case in ten thousand, even one hundred thousand, goes wrong. It happens though. Take your business, for example. A customer comes into your garage and he has a problem with his car. You think you know what the problem is so you buy a part to fix the car. You expect that part to be OK, no? And then the part turns out to be bad. Or maybe that's not the problem at all, and you needed to do something quite different to the car to fix it. You know what I mean? Whose fault is it? Is it your fault because you did not see what was the problem? Is it the company who sold you the part because some schmuck in some plant in some other country did not care enough to make the part properly in the first place? Or maybe it's the driver of the car who does not follow your instructions when you give it back to him? Not that it matters. If the driver has an accident and kills himself, or even kills someone else because the car is not right, who is at fault? The mechanic, the manufacturer, the driver? It is the same in the drug industry. We make things to help people get better, but sometimes something goes wrong, that is all."

"Well, I understand that. But what if your boss is on your back and tells you to hurry up and he makes you do a lousy job, and then the driver has an accident. We're always being pushed to finish a job quickly so we can get on with another. I bet that doesn't happen in your company."

"You're wrong, darling. It happens with us too. We have to produce a new drug quickly and we are forced to cut corners. We have to launch the product before the competition because we are quite often producing pretty much the same drug for the same problem. So we don't test a new drug long enough or carefully enough, or we oversell it to the doctors. We tell them the new drug is going to cure anything, everything, because we want them to prescribe the drug, and they are mostly too busy to check what we say carefully. And then patients get worse, not better, or they get better for a while and then they get hooked on our drug and they have to take stronger and stronger doses until it does not work any more, and then the patient is in real trouble. And so it goes on. The whole drug industry is full of problems and lots of funny business, and I'm very sick of it."

Still holding onto her hand, all Ron could say was, "Wow!"

"Wow is right, darling. And right now the pressure is increasing. H & H want us to make brand new drugs, breakthrough stuff, none of this me-too nonsense. They want to compete with the big boys and they are going to put big money into human ethicals. So Julian Horne decides to retire at the end of the month and Brian is going to be promoted into his job. He does not want it, our Brian. I do not blame him. But he and Gretl are sort of stuck here, he tells me, so he will try it out for a while and see how it goes. And they also want me to become a team leader. Everyone is going to belong to a team from now on. People who are not in a team will be fired, or they will be transferred to another laboratory where they will join a team. Everything is going to be organized for results, Paul Ruffin tells us. We produce or we are out, all of us, including him. Maybe it is time I did something else, something different. What do you think, darling?" she asked Ron, her hand gently stroking his arm.

"I don't know, sweetheart. They pay you a heap of money – four, five times what I make. It takes some beating. No new business is going to pay you anything like that for a year or two. The opportunity costs, as they taught me at college, just aren't there. If I were you, I'd stay in your job for as long as you can, even if you have to work a lot harder than you do now. And then all your close friends are there: Gretl and Brian, Michelle and Armand, others, you know. These are hard things to give away – money and people."

"Money we can make, and good friends we never lose. Just because Tony no longer works at H & H does not mean we will stop seeing him and Gloria. The question has to do with quality of worklife, no? I do not have it any more with H & H. We are going to become part of a large factory where performing and producing is all that matters. This is a good time to think of other things, even if, in the short term, there are some money losses. So what, as long as we are having fun, we are building something up, we are working with people we like, even love."

"Oho!" Ron stood and drank his port in one gulp. He went to the bar to refill his glass. "I think I know what you want to do. But don't do it for me, Bee. Sure, things are going well for us now, but what if they don't in two or three years. Sure, we like living and sleeping together, but what if we don't like working together? What if I want to do something else in a few years' time, or you get tired of the business, or it doesn't go well and you lose all your money? So many things can go wrong, Bee. Sure, it would be a great opportunity for me to go into business for myself and that's what I want to do. But I can't do it on your money. I can't let you do it, quit your job, take all your money, borrow a heap more from a bank, get into debt, and then maybe lose the lot because the idea of spare parts trucks is not such a smart one after all."

"You listen to me, Ronny. This is not something I dreamed up today. I have been thinking about your idea for months. I think it is a winner and, if we win, we can go into franchising, selling the special computer software you have developed, training franchisees, all these things. Do not forget, I have experience in wholesaling, good experience. I can be a real help to you. In a few years, Ronny, we could be rich and you will have done it, and I will have helped you do it. Sure, there is some risk. You or I could get sick. A million and one things could go wrong. But as long as we go on loving each other, as long as we believe in each other, and as long as we are having fun, little else matters. I do not have these things in H & H any more. It is time for a change. I am ready. You are ready. We must do it, Ronny, now, that is all."

Ron gulped down the remainder of his port and sat back, shutting his eyes as he did when he wanted to focus on some problem. Through clenched teeth, he muttered, "Why don't you phone Gloria and see if they can come tomorrow night? And then the others. Maybe we can talk this through with them over dinner. Brian, Armand, Tony, the girls. They're our closest friends and I trust them. They'll give us good advice. And then we must talk to the bank, a good lawyer, a good accountant, suppliers, a few other people, before you make any decision about your job. We've both waited all our lives to go into business for ourselves, so a week or two longer won't make much difference. What do you say?" He opened his eyes, sat up, took her hands in his, and gave her the smile she had come to recognize whenever he wanted to make love to her.

She squeezed his hands hard. "I think we should make love first, my darling. There will be plenty of time after that to make telephone calls."

Chapter 17

10.45 p.m., Saturday, 2 March

"It sounds like something I would choose if I wanted to go into business for myself and I had your skills and experience," Brian observed to Britt and Ron. "It's small enough to manage, but it has enormous potential for growth, and many other good things in its favour. In fact, I can only see the positive aspects of the venture, and few disadvantages. What do you say, Armand?"

Armand sat back in his chair and folded his arms across his chest. It was a pose they knew he assumed when he was about to express his final and irrevocable opinion on a particular subject. "I also like the idea and I think you should pursue it. However, I do not have to tell you the biggest danger for a new business is being undercapitalized. You must have enough money to withstand early disappointments. I have some knowledge of such things. My brother, Jules, has gone broke two times, both times because he thought he would get enough business in the first year of operations to cover his expenses. Well, it mostly does not happen that way. Make sure you can afford not to pay yourselves anything for the first year and maybe even make a small loss on top."

"You're too pessimistic, Armand," Tony broke in. "And you're frightening the hell out of poor Ron. From the look on his face, I bet you he's counting the money Beebee will have forgone by not being with H & H. But, in the final analysis, Ron," he turned to the young man at the head of the table, who sat with his head thrown back, eyes shut, gripping the arms of his chair tightly, "it comes down to a matter of personal choice, Beebee's and yours. Materially, Beebee's in a very solid position. She's free of debt and has no responsibilities, she has an excellent asset in this town house and will also have a healthy sum of ready cash when she leaves H & H, and, most importantly, she has extremely useful experience in a similar type of business. I can't comment on the viability of the computer software you've created, but if it's half as good as you tell us, you also bring to the table some critical expertise and experience. In fact, let's face it, without you, the idea would not be feasible."

Tony paused for effect. He was enjoying himself, his legal training adding substance to his thoughts. "Psychologically, with regard to giving up the security of one's job, being prepared to take risks, and so on, I think you'll all agree that Beebee's more than ready. She's probably been ready for a radical change in her lifestyle for some time. As for you, Ron, you've probably been ready for ever. You're too bright to want to work for someone else. Based on these considerations, therefore, I agree with Brian and Armand – you should make the move. I can almost guarantee you'll have no trouble getting a sizeable loan from the government's Small Business Bank on very favourable terms. So here's to both of you with our very best wishes. We'll be rooting for you every step of the way." He raised his glass and invited the other five guests at the dining table to toast their hosts.

"Incidentally, you two entrepreneurs, what are you going to call the company?" Gretl asked.

"I have not thought about this yet. But we are open to suggestions." Beebee looked across the table at Ron, his face tense, small beads of perspiration on his upper lip. "Ron, do you have something in mind? My Ronny always has something in mind about everything," she explained with great conviction.

"Sweetheart, I've thought about it a little, but I think we should wait 'til you're sure this is what you want to do." He started to wipe his mouth with his hand, then remembered in time and brought his linen serviette from his lap to his face, mopping his forehead and his mouth, and running a finger round his collar as if to ease the pressure.

Michelle, ever conscious of tension in people around her, cut in quickly. "Maybe it is time for us to let Beebee and Ron look into this matter a little more carefully between themselves. We are all agreed it is a very good idea and it should be a great success, non? Now I want to hear from Tony about the help he is getting from the consultants. I want to understand what it is they do."

"Do you honestly want to go into all that, Michelle?" Gloria interposed quickly, looking anxiously at Tony, who had visibly stiffened at the thought of having to talk about his job search activities. "This is all Tony has been doing since he . . . well, you know." She did not want to be specific about his forced retirement. "I'm sure he would probably much rather not have to talk about it after such a thoroughly relaxing evening."

"*Mais oui*, Gloria, I *would* like to know about these things and I think Tony should tell us about them. I may be wrong, but I think it will do him good to tell his closest friends what he has done and how he feels about them."

Tony held up his hand to Gloria, indicating that he could deal with this matter. "Michelle is perfectly right, dear. I think it would do me good to talk about my experiences with the consultants, if it's OK with everyone?" He looked around the table, trying to gauge the degree of interest in the faces of his friends.

Ron cut in. "Hey, Tony, I'm with Michelle. I sure want to know about these things. After all, if you can't tell us what it's all about, no one can."

Tony took a deep breath and closed his eyes, as if he was

about to dive into a bottomless pool. He let his breath out slowly, looked quickly at the faces round the table and grimaced. "Very well. First of all, let me tell you, there is nothing more soul destroying for a man who has worked all his life than suddenly to find himself out of a job. The first three or four days after Paul Ruffin called me into his office to tell me I was redundant, I'd get up at the usual hour and in the usual hurry, and get myself ready for work like I've been doing for over thirty years. And then I'd realize I didn't have to get out of bed. I could lie around a little longer – a lot longer if I chose to. Hell, I could stay in bed all day for that matter. After all, there was absolutely no need for me to get up. There was nothing I had to do today that couldn't be done tomorrow, the day after, maybe never."

He paused and looked directly at Armand. "Let me add this, however. In retrospect, Paul could not have been nicer about this sorry business. I was angry when he told me and I wanted to lash out – at him, at H & H, at anybody who was vaguely connected with putting me out to grass after all my years of service and at the peak of my professional competence. He remained silent the whole time while I raved and ranted about the injustice of it all. Then he patiently drew my attention back to the sheet on which were printed my redundancy entitlements, which were very generous. And he urged me to make good use of the consultants, who he said could be of great help, if I would let them. Finally, when I'd talked myself out, a good half hour later, he told me I could come and see him at any time if I wanted to talk to him about anything. Furthermore, he would be very comfortable writing the best possible reference for me if it would help me in any way."

He looked at his wife who was sitting across from him, her face drawn as she relived these first few days. "During those first few mornings, there were moments of very real despondency and despair, let me tell you. Anyway, Gloria would come and sit on the side of the bed, give me a big hug, wave a long list of things that needed to be done around the house and the garden, order me out of bed and literally bully me into getting on with life. And then, the next week, each morning she made me get dressed as if I was going to work, and she drove me to the consultants so that I could begin the search process. I owe her everything my friends, perhaps even my sanity, for there were moments, you know, when I thought life was no longer worth living . . ." He looked down, blinking to stifle his emotion.

Beebee leaned over at once and gave him a big kiss on the cheek, leaving a vivid imprint of her lips. "Gloria, darling, you must make sure that he never washes his face again. These are the lips that would have launched a thousand ships, if I had lived in another time."

"Well, sweetheart, you don't," Ron interrupted. "You make sure you wash your face, Tony, or you'll never be the same. Look what's happened to me since she started putting these lipstick marks all over me . . .!"

"Enough, Ronny, or they will all go home to leave me to put more lipstick all over you."

"OK, you two. Stop putting ideas in our heads," Brian broke in. "Tony, please continue."

"Let me describe, first of all, the set-up in the consultants' rented premises downtown. Imagine a huge, open barn of a place with about three dozen good-sized cubicles placed randomly about the floor – I mean randomly. There is no apparent design except that each cubicle seems to make the occupant feel it's his or her very own – which means that they obviously went to a great deal of trouble to place the cubicles where they are. In any event, in each cubicle there's a small desk with a bookcase on top, a comfortable desk chair, an armchair for a visitor, a one-drawer filing cabinet, and a phone that goes through a switchboard where they take messages for you. On the desk, they provide you with everything you might need: computer, stapler, tape dispenser, ballpoint pens, pencils, pads and paper, envelopes, that sort of thing. If you want anything else, all you need do is ask and, if they don't have it in stock, they'll buy it. There are three photocopiers and three printers on one side wall. On the opposite wall are five offices where the consultants are located. Their doors are always open, unless someone wants some privacy. Any questions so far?"

Tony took a sip of wine while he waited for questions. There were none. He had their complete attention. "In that case, let me continue. The consultants encouraged me to come to work every day as if this was my job – and it is, of course. My current job is to find employment, and I must develop a mind-set, a focus, where this is what I do full time every day of the week, including Saturday and Sunday, if I want to. Within the first hour of my arrival, after going through a quite involved registration procedure, I was allotted an adviser, and a cubicle. Jerry Croft gave me a conducted tour of the premises and then went through the routine of explaining what I could do and what resources I could tap into. There were secretaries, a video centre, two training rooms, five small but tastefully furnished interview offices where we could meet with potential employers, a canteen, that sort of thing. I was encouraged to make the cubicle exclusively mine by bringing in my favourite pictures or posters, whatever would make me feel comfortable. There were keys to the top drawer of the desk and the filing cabinet." Tony stopped. "Please interrupt me at any time. You know me. If I'm going to explain, I'm going to do it as thoroughly as I can, so make the most of it, folks. In the meantime, Ron, how about some more of that excellent wine?"

He continued while Ron went about topping up everyone's glass. "As soon as I had settled in and made a list of the additional things I would need, I went to see Jerry again. He gave me a run down on what I was to do for the next few days. Most of it was training: how to track down every job possibility, including jobs I had never thought I might want to do; how to prepare a CV and a covering letter; how to use the phone; how to handle an interview; how to make a formal presentation; you name it, it's on tap, with supporting written, audio and video material. In addition, there is a comprehensive library of technical books on job-search matters which is at our disposal. We can make any number of phone calls anywhere, we can use the photocopier as much as we want, we can work as early or as late as we like. The honour system applies, we were told, and it seems to work well. No one abuses it."

Ron, who was taking out the cork from a new bottle of wine, couldn't contain himself. "Wow, Tony, what a set up. It must be costing H & H a mint to make all this available to employees who've been laid off. Is it open to everyone, or just executives like you?"

"It's there for everyone who has been forcibly retired and, yes, it's very professional and I expect it's costing H & H a mint." He took an appreciative sip of the wine, and held his glass up to the light. "Ron, you know how to pick a good one."

"I'm learning. Bee's the one who's forcing me to understand these things. She thinks we're going to be rich one day and we'll have a large house, with servants, all these good things. And we'll have to entertain the captains of industry. Me, give me a business that pays the overdraft and an occasional holiday in the sun, a few close friends who enjoy good things, that's all I want."

"You will want more, Ron. Our appetites for better things grow with our experiences, you wait and see," Armand interjected, his arms still crossed on his chest. "*Eh bien*, Tony, *mon ami*, it is clear that Paul Ruffin and H & H are trying to do their best for you. I am glad. How long is that service available?"

"For as long as it takes any of us to find appropriate jobs. In just the last week or so, over half the retirees have found jobs. Mind you, most were in non-supervisory positions. Nonetheless, the consultants are doing a great job. They're true professionals. I expect it will be a little harder for me to find something at my level, but I'm beginning to feel much better about the whole business. Not that I'm enjoying it, mind you. But at least I'm getting the kind of help I need. I hate to think what I'd have done if that consultancy hadn't been laid on for us. Hell, it must be twenty-five years since I had an interview for a job. I'd be thrashing about like a fish out of water if it wasn't for them.

And I can't imagine what it would cost me to obtain professional advice at that level, even if I was smart enough to think about making use of such an organization in the first place. I tell you what, if one has to be retrenched, it makes life considerably easier to have such a service immediately available."

"Tony, I'm so happy for you and I do hope you'll find something suitable very soon," Gretl told him. She looked at her wristwatch. "Brian, do you know what time it is? We have to rescue Kimmy from that boy next door. I still think he knows too much and she knows too little. I know I sound like an overanxious mother, Beebee and Ron, but we'll have to run. This has been a wonderful evening, with so much good news, for both of you, and for Tony too. I'm so glad we had nothing else planned for tonight . . ."

Chapter 18

11.00 a.m., Monday, 16 March

Brian Curtis was running late for the weekly Communications Committee meeting. He walked into Paul's office just as he was handing out a folder to each of the other three members of the group. Paul waved him in with a relieved smile, symbolically wiping his brow. They were sitting at the round table in the middle of Paul's large office. This was where he and Paul always sat whenever he had reason to see him in his office or whenever they had a small group meeting like the present one.

The office had been radically transformed since Norman Coles's departure. Gone was the huge mahogany desk which had sat ponderously in the centre of the room and immediately in front of the large landscape window. Also gone was the arrangement of four leather armchairs placed squarely around the modern glass coffee table. Not that Brian had ever been invited to sit in one of them. By all accounts, neither had any other employee in the division. These armchairs were strictly for visiting dignitaries, board members, people who were likely to advance Norman Coles's career. Whenever he had been summoned to Norman's office, he had always been told to sit in one of the three uncomfortable low-backed wooden chairs facing the desk, the light from the window falling directly in his eyes so that Norman Coles's head often seemed to be surrounded by a halo. Gone also from the walls were all the mementos and pictures of Norman with important people.

Instead, in the corner, Paul had placed a small grey steel desk, with one four-drawer filing cabinet jammed between the desk and the wall. On the desk was the standard issue computer available to every employee in the division, and a phone. The dominant feature in the room was the single round table and six of the comfortable chairs which Paul had borrowed from the conference room next door. The only items of luxury were three original lithographs of famous Italian churches that hung on the wall above the desk, and a very large rectangular Persian rug under the table and chairs. Otherwise, the room was stripped of all pretension to being anything but the office of a busy senior executive.

"I was beginning to think something had happened to you over the weekend, Brian. Glad you've made it, anyway." Brian hurriedly sat in his usual place at Paul's right hand. "We have to make some hard decisions about a very important matter," Paul continued. He handed Brian a folder with his name written on it in bold black letters, and immediately beneath, "STRICTLY CONFIDENTIAL" in red.

"Isabel, I don't want any minutes of this meeting. I want you, John, Ingrid and Brian to concentrate solely on the issues we have to resolve." He opened his copy of the folder and studied it for a moment. "This folder contains the names, positions, salary ranges and current salaries of the people who are going to be urged to regard H & H as their permanent employer and the HE Division as their permanent place of work. I have final and definitive confirmation from head office there will be no further cuts or changes in the composition of our teams. Our only concern from now on is to settle the personnel side of the organization and get everyone focused on income-generating research."

Paul closed his folder with deliberation. "The list includes all those who have been retained from the old AgriBus division, have transferred from other locations in H & H, will join us from H & H in the near future, or have already joined us from outside. It excludes people who have resigned for their own good reasons and will be leaving us by the end of the month. I have in mind a handful of people like Dr Britt Berghoff. I could not persuade her and the others to continue with us. I am naturally very disappointed. They will be sorely missed. I know they would have made a very real contribution to our research programme."

Brian opened his folder and began to run his finger down the list. "Don't go through the folder yet, Brian," Paul interrupted quietly. "You can do that later. There are no surprises. This is more or less what we decided should be our new structure at the Operating Committee meeting three weeks ago. What is critical is that we begin to assure everyone in the division that they now have stable positions and can stop spending valuable time looking over their shoulders. Provided we don't make any terminal mistakes – in which case my job, most of all, will be on the block – we're going to run for the foreseeable future with the people on that list. By foreseeable future, I mean the remainder of this year at least."

Brian looked cynically at Paul. He had heard that story before on several occasions. Over the past six weeks, the division had been drastically shorn of all but the most essential employees. They were now down to the bone in the two remaining operating departments, Research and Development. Marketing had disappeared as a functioning department, with the exception of a small team in sales liaison who were mostly pharmacists. Colin Marks and a dozen or so product specialists had been transferred to the newly formed International Marketing Division for human ethicals at reduced status and pay. The remainder had found other employment or been forcibly retired. There had also been a sizeable movement of scientists and support technicians to teams working on a variety of promising drugs at different research facilities around the organization. The 40 per cent or so that were left in Research and Development from the former AgriBus division – those who had decided for their own good reasons not to leave – had been formed into three teams and were now working solely on a dozen or so drugs that had the greatest potential for commercial success.

Brian looked across at Ingrid Andersen, whose face registered very real concern as she fingered the corners of the folder. Colin Marks had made an excellent choice when he had proposed her as the person from marketing most likely to help them frame and execute communication policy. Like the rest of that small committee, Brian had come to respect Ingrid's public relations abilities, as well as her common sense. Right now, if Brian understood her facial expression correctly, knowing what everyone was earning was making her uncomfortable, as it did Brian. This was not the kind of information he wanted to take out of Paul's office and lock away in his desk. In confirmation, she shook her head at him, indicating with her eyes the folder in front of her.

"OK, you two," said Paul, looking from Ingrid to Brian and back again, and pretending he didn't understand what was going on between them. "Enough of these non-verbal messages. You go first, Brian."

"Well, Paul, I've never ever had such an explosive document in my possession. I think Ingrid is also concerned." He looked at her, inviting her to comment.

"Exactly, Dr Ruffin," she stated, her face pale, blonde hair and blue eyes nodding vigorous approval. "These are matters for very senior managers and the Human Resource Department."

"Why?" Paul asked, accepting resignedly her habitual acknowledgment of his status and position. At times like these, she was very Swedish.

She hesitated, looking at Brian for help.

Paul held up his hand. "I want Ingrid to answer, please, Brian."

Brian shrugged, intimating with that noncommittal gesture of his that he was confident she could look after herself.

She hesitated for the briefest of moments. "I do not believe people like other people to know how much they earn," she told them, the high-pitched Swedish accent and tone coming through more strongly than usual.

"Why?" Paul persisted, a look of genuine interest on his face.

"That is my experience on such matters. I also remember the classes on salary administration in my human resource course. Our instructor recommended not to make this information available. For example, I do not think it is right I should know your salary. If you want to tell me, that is different."

Paul did not hesitate. "I want you to turn to page four of the folder. About half way down, you will see the name Ruffin. It tells you what my base salary is. It does not tell you what extras are part of my total pay packet. That's because these are only usually available to senior executives or prospective employees who have something special to bring to the bartering table. Let me tell you what these extras are. I receive an allowance for a fully maintained motorcar. I supplement this allowance from my salary to drive a Jaguar. I just happen to like Jaguars. The company's allowance is . . ."

Ingrid was now clearly agitated. "Dr Ruffin, please. I did not use you as an example because I wanted to know how much money you make. It does not interest me. I am sure they pay you what you deserve . . ."

"But that's the point precisely, Ingrid. I believe I deserve it and I intend to prove it over the next few months to my superiors and, most of all, to everyone else in the division. After all, how can anyone justify his or her pay by making a big secret of it?" He turned to Brian. "I bet you and Gretl have asked yourselves what H & H pay me to do this job. And I bet you both guessed I earn a lot more than I do."

Brian looked up from the folder. "You're not wrong, Paul, unless a good proportion of your total pay package is in hidden benefits and perks."

"There you go then." Paul turned once more to Ingrid. "I don't know why your instructor advised secrecy. The latest trend is to make salaries open to anyone who wants to know. It stops guessing, which is almost always on the upside and makes people angry because they feel they are being underpaid relative to others in similar positions. And that goes for all sorts of other practices within a company. The more people know about what's going on, good and bad, the more likely they are to understand where they fit in, the importance of the job they do, and why they must always do the best they can. Think of it, Ingrid. The most bureaucratic organization in the world, the public service, make no secret about salaries and never seem to have problems on that issue. Let me assure you that, very soon, that list before you will be available to anyone who wants to know how much other people earn. Which brings me to the subject at hand. What do we do to spread the word that the bad times are finally behind us and the good times lie ahead?"

"You're talking about mounting a public relations campaign to sell the division under H & H management to its employees. Or have I got it wrong?" Brian asked.

"You've hit the nail on the head, Brian."

"You do realize that you have an enormous credibility problem?" Brian continued.

"I most certainly do. And that's what we have to begin to deal with this morning, and over the coming weeks, months. That does not mean a return to the comfortable club atmosphere that was prevalent in AgriBus days, but I'm not talking about a sweatshop either. Somehow, we have to convince the people out there that we must all pull together because there's important work to do. I want everyone to feel my sense of excitement at having the opportunity to do something useful, to contribute, to help expand our horizons of knowledge. I want everyone to tell themselves on Sunday night, 'Whoopee! Tomorrow's Monday. I'm going back to work'. I know it sounds utopian, but there are organizations around the world where employees look forward to going to work every day. I'd like us to devise a change programme which will make this atmosphere possible." Paul sat back in his chair and waited for a reaction.

A full minute passed during which Ingrid Andersen continued

to run her fingers around the corners of the folder, Isabel Esporanta sat back in her chair, her eyes shut, John Trury was doodling on his pad, his brow knitted in concentration, and Brian Curtis held his head in his hands, elbows on the table, his eyes fixed on the folder before him.

Paul brought them back. "All right. Let's reduce the size of the immediate exercise. We have one vital piece of information which the workforce needs to hear, that is, job security. How do we get that across without appearing sanctimonious at one end of the scale – as in, 'Hey, people, guess what? No one else is getting fired from now on. Aren't we being good' – to menacing at the other – as in, 'Hey, people, guess what? A slight change in direction. We'll let you keep your jobs for the present. But don't let me catch you making mistakes or you'll be out on your ear like all the rest'?"

Another full minute passed and still nothing was said, until Paul, with a hint of exasperation in his voice, snapped, "All right. Why don't we leave it here for this week. But I want us all to come in next Monday . . ."

John Trury interrupted him. "The problem is that such an announcement, on its own, in the present climate, will be interpreted in either of those two ways – and in every other way in between! It's a lose-lose situation. I think the notion of job security is only one part of a total change programme. Both Isabel and I have been part of takeovers before, but we've never had to deal with these sensitive human resource issues. What I'm trying to say, Paul, is that I think we need professional help. I think we should have the human resource experts from head office come and show us how to do it."

"I agree," Isabel spoke out in her firm low-pitched voice. "This is a tricky area. I think you should go to head office and spend some time with the HR people. The problem is that it needs to be done as soon as possible. The longer it takes for the people out there to come to terms with their changed situation, the more difficult it will be to bring them back to where we want them to be, where they need to be. It will take real expertise to change them into 'Whoopee' people who can work together and produce results."

Once again, there was total silence as Paul, Brian and Ingrid looked at each other.

"In principle, I don't disagree with either of you," Brian interjected finally. "What always worries me about so-called head office experts coming into an organization is that they think they know everything. Every organization has funny little twists and turns, it's called 'culture', and these experts often ride roughshod over these items. And then they walk away when things don't work out and leave us to clear up the mess."

Paul looked at Ingrid. "Your turn. What do you think?"

"I think Isabel and John are right about bringing in experts. I did a course in organizational change some years ago and one of the conclusions was that an experienced change agent can do a great deal of good. I also understand why Brian is being careful. I suppose, Dr Ruffin, it is an excellent idea to ask for help, but make sure the tail does not wag the dog, if you understand what I mean."

"I know exactly what you mean, Ingrid. And thank you, John and Isabel, for reminding me that we could do with some help. Sometimes people in my position think we can do everything by ourselves. And thank you, Brian and Ingrid, for reminding me not to delegate and abdicate on this matter. I'm going to have to monitor the change process as closely as possible. Leave it with me. I'll come back to you next Monday and report back. Before we break up, let me add one last thought. I want this committee to continue working with me on these matters. As you've just seen, I need your help as much as I need outside expertise. I think it's going to be an interesting time for us all over the next few months, so hang in there with me, team."

Part V
A new beginning

Chapter 19

11.45 a.m., Monday, 18 May

Paul leafed through the small pile of job descriptions once again. "I seem to have mislaid Norman Earle's job description, Ingrid. I'd better find it. Wouldn't do to leave our new head of toxicology out of the team development process, even if he is a pedantic pain in the neck."

"Don't talk to me about it, Paul. You have no idea how badly I miss Britt Berghoff," muttered Brian Curtis.

"I tried, Brian, believe me, I tried. But she wanted to go. I wish her and that Ron of hers the very best of luck."

"Take my copy, Dr Ruffin," Ingrid cut in, hurriedly looking through her folder. "Here it is. I'll make another copy for myself after the meeting."

There was a brittle edge to Ingrid Andersen's voice which caused Paul to look apprehensively at her. "That takes care of stage one for all senior staff and team leaders. I expect you'll want to start on the first line supervisors next. Can you manage on your own, Ingrid?"

"I must, Dr Ruffin. The job of Human Resource manager in

a division this size is OK for just one person. I have to do it, that is all."

Again, he was conscious of the break in her voice. She looked tired. But then, they all were. Many factors were involved in rebuilding the personnel structure of the division, and at the same time getting everyone focused on their mission. "I thought you might like to take on the job, Ingrid, but I must not ask you to do the impossible. Interviewing these twenty-two supervisors and preparing their PDs is going to take some doing, without everything you already have on your plate. I want you to tell me if you need help."

Isabel Esporanta interrupted him. "Ingrid and I have an arrangement, Paul. If she feels she wants some help, all she has to do is ask."

She too had acquired a sharpness in her voice. He wondered if he was working them all too hard, his inner group on the Communications Committee. It was time to take some tension out of the meeting, a task he enjoyed particularly and at which he was usually very successful. He fixed Isabel with a stern look "Ask who? You? Are you saying you don't have enough to do?" Paul inquired of her, giving her his mischievous grin.

"That's not it at all . . ." she replied defensively, missing the humour in his face.

"I'm also available," John Trury said, quickly realizing that Paul was playing one of his "let's cool it" games.

"You too? I thought you had more than enough to do without delving into Human Resource matters." He turned to Ingrid once more. "Mrs Andersen, I want you to know that all this assistance when you snap your fingers makes me look bad. Now, what I would like you to do . . ."

"Paul," Brian cut in, smiling faintly. "I think we ought to keep going, however well intentioned you are. What's next on your agenda?"

He scowled at Brian. "Did I ever tell you, Brian Curtis, you're a real spoilsport. I just thought it would help to ease the tension a little if I teased our two very intense fellow committee members." He looked at the others around the table. "However, if that's the way you all want to play it, let's be serious." He sat back in his chair, crossed his arms on his chest and lowered his head reflectively. "I want for a few moments to discuss the Advisory Committee. I haven't yet shared with you my progress with that group, but I'm beginning to wonder whether they're ever going to tell me if there is anything wrong anywhere in the division. I can't believe that all 180-odd people are deliriously happy with everything."

Brian held up his hand to get Paul's attention. "You'll remember, Paul, I was away at a pathology conference when the head office consultant suggested you create the Advisory Committee. As I understand it, its purpose is to provide a pipeline from all levels of the division directly to you through elected representatives. I know elections were held and three of the people in Development are on that committee. I also know that you meet the second Monday of each month. But I've never clearly understood what the committee is specifically supposed to do. Is this an appropriate moment to tell me about it, without wasting everyone's time?"

Paul nodded his approval. "Now that you mention it, I think it's an excellent opportunity to make sure we're all on the same wavelength on that issue. Yes, I remember now. You were away at a conference, and then you couldn't be here the following week, by which time the decision about creating the Advisory Committee had been made and the details finalized without any input from you. Briefly, the idea is based on the difficulty every CEO has in getting reliable and timely information about problems which affect the efficiency and effectiveness of his or her organization. In simple terms, I need a mechanism by which everyone in the division can bypass the chain of command and bring any work-related problems they're having to my attention, so that I can act on them as quickly as possible. I also need another mechanism which makes it possible for me to share with everyone in the division what problems I'm having at the top, and involve them in helping me find solutions."

Paul shuffled through his file and produced a one-page document. "Read this when you have a moment," he told Brian, handing him the sheet. "Unlike the other committees, it was decided that the Advisory Committee must consist of employees elected by their peers to represent their interests. In that sense, it makes available to every member of the division a democratic and impartial platform through which any grievance can be heard and settled promptly, whether that grievance comes from the top or the bottom, or anywhere in between. It entails two-way communication. In terms of downward communication, I share with the members what problems I have been having during the prior month, and what problems I think I will have during the coming month. In terms of upward communication, each representative must hold at least one meeting with his electorate every month and report to me any specific concerns any of them is having. Minutes must be distributed to everyone in the division as soon after the monthly meeting as possible. In theory, the Advisory Committee makes all sorts of important information readily available to everyone so that decisions can be made on any issue that needs immediate attention. In practice, it's not working out that way."

Isabel, who had been only peripherally involved in the creation of the committee, looked confused. "What's gone wrong?" she asked.

"It just hasn't come together, that's what's gone wrong," he replied. "Maybe my expectations are too high. I don't know. Let me see if I can tell you what isn't happening. I've had two meetings since the elections. In the first one, we went through our objectives very carefully and very thoroughly. I then gave them a list of problems I had, ranging from policy issues like, 'Were we totally clear about our objectives, and, if not, what should we do about it?' to mundane matters like 'Was the menu in the staff canteen sufficiently varied?' I thought that meeting went very well."

He pursed his lips as he usually did when he was unhappy. "I had my second meeting last week. I went through my list of problems, present and projected, and waited for their suggestions. What I received was a resounding silence. I mean, you'd imagine there'd be something from the eight people there. Nothing, *niente, rien*. So I told them to think about the issues and come back with any suggestions they thought might help. Nothing aggressive, you understand, although I could have torn off a few heads. I then went into the upward communication bit. What problems were they having that I should know about? And again, nothing. I asked them if they had conducted their meetings with their electorates? Yes. How had these meetings gone? Very well. Had anyone brought up a problem which needed my attention? No. Did this mean there were no problems in the division? Silence. That's what's gone wrong, Isabel. So, team, what do I do? And don't give me any more of that silence routine. I expect some real input from you."

They remained thoughtful for a full minute while Paul drummed his fingers impatiently on the arm of his chair. Finally, he burst out, "What's going on? Is there a conspiracy of silence in the division? Brian, speak to me."

Brian shrugged. "I frankly don't know what to tell you."

"John Trury?"

John hesitated for a moment, his head bent over his notepad. He gestured with both hands, indicating to Paul, who was watching him closely, that he was about to get what he so much wanted – both barrels of unadulterated home truths. "I think you're expecting developments too quickly. Let's face it, Paul. The division's been decimated. All sorts of promises were made at the time of the takeover and many were broken. To top it off, the people who are left have been warned that if they don't produce, heads will begin to roll again. They've also been told there'll be no more retrenchments and, sure enough, there haven't been in the last two months. But realistically there *can't* be any more retrenchments – the division's down to the bone, and they know it. Now you want them to tell you what problems they're having so that you can fix them. Suddenly you're all heart, dripping with the milk of human kindness. But there's a catch, as in everything they've come to expect from H & H. You want them to help *you* solve *your* problems. And it's all orchestrated against a background of democratic music which fools no one. Is it any wonder you're getting silence."

Paul had remained perfectly still during this plain speaking, his head still down on his chest. He blinked and raised his eyes to look directly at John. "Are you saying the Advisory Committee is a mistake?"

"Not at all. But I am saying you're expecting everything to fall into place far too quickly. They don't trust you yet. You're going to have to earn their confidence before they open up to you."

Paul turned away from John, frowning. "Isabel?"

"I think the Advisory Committee is the centrepiece of your change strategy. But it is only one of the many pieces which must come together, as you've reminded us on a number of occasions. As the other pieces begin to contribute to the building of faith in you and H & H, they'll begin to tell you what you want to know. It will come, but it will take time."

"How long?"

"A few months, maybe as far as the end of the year."

"Ingrid?"

"This is what your head office consultant told us. It will take time. The whole change programme is very ambitious, he said, more ambitious than in any other part of H & H. But if you do it right, he said, you will turn the division into a dynamo. I remember his words very clearly, Dr Ruffin. And he also said you will have many disappointments. This is your first one. But I know you will succeed because you are determined to succeed. And we will be right behind you."

Paul nodded and smiled at her. "Brian? Back to you."

"I think they've said it all, Paul. John reminded you that the division is like a wounded animal. You can't expect it to forget its wounds and respond positively to your first command. Isabel told you that the Advisory Committee is important. However, it won't function properly until a lot of other pieces are on the table and interacting to produce the synergy you're looking for. And Ingrid has said that those pieces won't fall into place without some frustrations, but that you must persist and keep pushing for change."

"So what do I do at the next meeting when they tell me no one in the division has a problem?"

"Hey!" Brian exclaimed. "You tell them it's wonderful, there are no problems and you look forward to the next meeting. Maybe the next month there will be something they want to bring to your attention."

"And what do I say when they tell me they have no suggestions for my problems?"

"You tell them it's a shame they have no ideas, but maybe they will at the next meeting."

"And what do I do when this goes on for another three or four months? Do you know how stupid I already feel? More to the point, do you know how stupid they'll think I am?"

"They might to begin with. But it won't last. These tests go with the territory, I remember you telling us."

"Some territory!" Paul exclaimed. "But, you're right, all of you. As Brian says, I'll have to keep pushing for change until I achieve what I want. In the meantime, will somebody tell me what we've achieved so far?"

Ingrid once again opened her folder and leafed through it. She produced *the change model* which the consultant had proposed they should use as the basis for creating a *high involvement workforce*. "With your permission, Dr Ruffin," as always, very correct, "I think we must all look at this model again to answer your question."

They all rummaged through their folders to find the model. Paul was the first to find his copy. "So what does it tell us? Apart from the preparation of the *guiding concepts and shared values* – which, incidentally, is still in circulation and has yet to be accepted – what have we completed so far? Let's take each of the nine characteristics in turn. What have we done about *leadership*?"

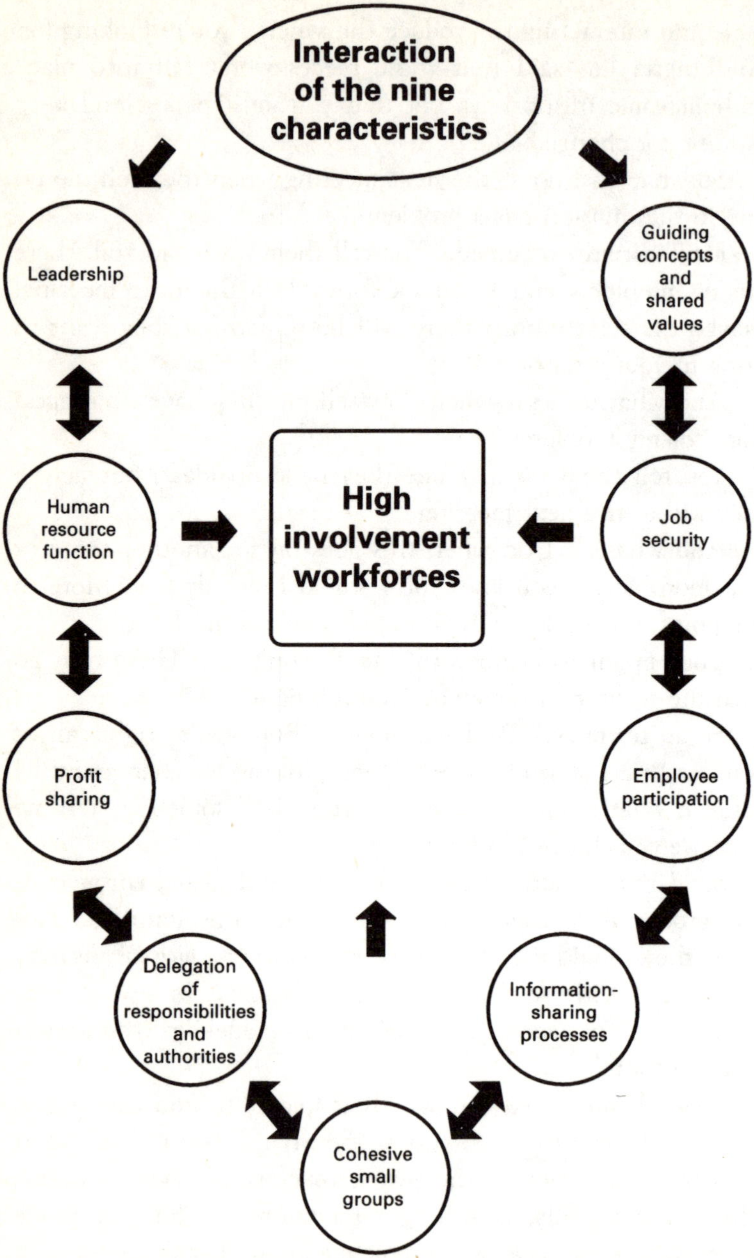

The change model

He looked around the table at the bent heads of his Communication Committee. "All right, let's take the next one, *human resource function*."

"I don't think it's meant to work that way, Paul," John Trury objected. "Ingrid and I discussed the model at some length with the consultant. He was quite specific that we should use the characteristics as guidelines and not as separate entities. He made an especially big point about the *interaction of the nine characteristics*. For example, you can't talk about needing *leadership* without acknowledging its interaction with *delegation of responsibilities and authorities, cohesive small groups, information sharing, employee participation*, in fact, every one of the other eight characteristics. They all hang together."

"All right. I understand that. But suppose my boss, the CEO of the new HE company visits me today and asks me what I'm doing to bring my workforce together. What do I tell him?"

Brian smiled thinly. "You give him a copy of the change model. Then you tell him we have a highly effective Human Resource function in the making. You tell him we have the beginnings of a programme to create *cohesive small groups*, which incorporates the *delegation of responsibilities and authorities*. You tell him we've structured a mechanism to encourage *employee participation*, we hope we continue to have *job security*, H & H willing, and we're looking around for an outside consultant who can provide the kind of *leadership* training which fits into the model. In fact, you can tell him, in two months, we've achieved a great deal and we propose to pursue the main objective of creating a *high involvement workforce* as vigorously as possible. If he asks you how long it will take to have such a *high involvement workforce* in the division, tell him our aim is to have all the pieces in place by the end of the year. If he asks you why it will take so long, you have two options: you can either tell him he's an ignorant clot who should go away and let you get on with your job, or you can repeat what John, Isabel and Ingrid just told you. Frankly, I would tell him the former."

Paul turned to Ingrid with the mischievous grin back on his

face. "As secretary of this committee, I hope you made a record of all that. I may need it before too long. On which note," he turned to the others, "having just given me a well-deserved lesson in patience and other good things, I think that's all I can take for one day. Keep up the good work, team. I need you to keep me on the straight and narrow path."

Chapter 20

1.00 p.m., Tuesday, 22 July

Gretl Curtis walked briskly into The Salad Bowl and looked around the cavernous dining room. It was surprisingly crowded for a Tuesday, in the middle of a supposed mini-recession. With so many unemployed, it didn't make sense for people to be lunching out in such numbers. But then, she had given up trying to understand the relationship between the state of the economy, disposable income, saving patterns, and the eating habits of the population.

She sighted Michelle Hernier at a table for four by the window, waving to attract her attention, and quickly threaded her way across the room. "*Ma chère*," Michelle called out, standing and giving Gretl a warm kiss on both cheeks, "I am so happy you are early. It seems an eternity since we last saw each other, I do not know why. And we have so much to talk about, just the two of us."

They sat opposite each other. Gretl replied, "I can tell you why very quickly, my dear. We've been going with our husbands to conferences, visits to head office, other company locations, all at the company's expense, first class, that's why."

"Is it not wonderful?" Michelle exclaimed. "AgriBus never treated Armand like that."

"But then, Michelle, AgriBus never required Armand, or Brian, for that matter, to work sixty- and seventy-hour weeks. Let me tell you, Brian is a new man. I have never seen him so excited about going to work."

"It is the same with Armand. I hear him singing and whistling 'La Marseillaise', 'La Vie en Rose', 'La Mer', his whole repertoire, in the shower every morning. And he is going to work so early. Even the children ask me, 'What is wrong with Papa?'. It is a long time since this has happened, let me tell you."

"There's no doubt in my mind, Michelle. Paul Ruffin has made all the difference. It certainly could never have been this way working with that self-seeking little dictator, Norman Coles. I remember Brian coming home some evenings and telling me he had come that close," indicating the narrow distance with thumb and forefinger, "to leaning across Norman's big desk and punching him on the nose. No, this is what it takes to get people up and running: a good boss who's excited about the work they're doing, and who treats his people well."

"But it is not just that, Gretl. There is so much else going on. Last week Armand told me he had just finished something he called a *team development exercise*, and he is now closer to his people than he thought possible. They think and work like a well-oiled team, he was saying. And that makes all the difference in the world, except I do not know what he means by this *team development exercise*, and he says he does not have the time to explain it to me."

"Easy. Brian explained it to me. You know Brian is a member of Paul's Communications Committee. They decide what goes on, and with whom, so he has to know about all these matters."

"*Ou-là-là*! I think you are very happy with your Brian."

"Michelle, I didn't mean it that way," and jokingly she made as if to slap her on the hand. "It's just that he has to know these aspects and he likes to explain them to me. He tells me that if I can understand what he's saying, then anyone else can. *Très* charming, my Brian. Anyway, if you want to know about that *team development exercise* business, I'll tell you, so long as you don't make funny remarks."

"I will not, I promise. Now tell me about this thing which they all seem to like so much."

"Stop me if there's something you don't understand."

She rummaged briefly through her handbag, found a pen and proceeded to draw a figure on her serviette.

Step 1 Specialist prepares job description (JD) with each manager, specifying all Responsibilities, Authorities and Accountabilities.

Step 2 Each manager discusses their JD with his or her immediate superior.

Step 3 Each manager discusses their JD with every immediate subordinate.

Step 4 Each manager and all his or her subordinates discuss their JDs.

Step 5 Discussion of the results of the OCAT Questionnaire.

"It consists of five steps. Let's say Armand is the one who is being put through this exercise. In the first step, Ingrid Andersen, the Human Resource manager, meets with Armand in his office, and he explains to her his job as manager of the Research Department. She makes sure he explains his job in three ways: responsibilities, authorities and accountabilities. Then she prepares the position description to Armand's satisfaction. Do you know what these three words mean?"

"*Mais oui*, Gretl," she replied too quickly.

"All right, smartypants, tell me what they mean."

"*Eh bien*! This is not an examination."

"You were the one who wanted to know."

"But not so well."

"Too late. What's the meaning of 'responsibilities'?"

"If you insist. All the different things you have to do to get your job done."

"Very good. I'm impressed."

"Thank you, *madame*."

"'Authorities'?"

"It is the amount of power you have to make decisions."

"Excellent. Go to the top of the class. Finally, 'accountabilities'."

"It is almost the same as responsibilities."

"Wrong. Go to the bottom of the class."

"Oh, very well! It is not the same as responsibilities. Armand is accountable for his responsibilities only if he has the power to make decisions, in other words, if he has the authority to decide how he does his job."

Gretl looked closely at her friend. "You're playing with me, Michelle. Armand explained these terms to you, didn't he?"

"No, he did not, I swear. But he gave me the instruction sheet for step one. That is all, *chérie*."

"In that case, you're cleverer than most of us, understanding what's on that sheet. You'll learn the next four steps very easily, I'm sure. So let me go through them quickly before the others arrive. Step two. Armand sits with his boss, Paul, and they go through the position description and make changes where necessary. Usually these changes are about the authorities Armand should have. For example, after his meeting with Paul, Brian found himself with some powers that he did not have before. Paul told him that, as manager of the Development Department, he now had the power to hire and fire, to spend money, and to travel, without having to get permission from him. And naturally, Paul now holds Brian accountable for not making bad decisions or abusing his powers. I think step two is very important for a manager at Brian's level. After all, he has over a hundred people who report to him, and millions of dollars' worth of equipment and animals. With Norman Coles, Julian Horne used to have to go to him for approval to buy anything. Anyway, that's all in the past."

"So what is step three?"

"Armand has to go through the same process – steps one and two – with all the people who report to him, one by one, giving a little of his power away to each of them."

"Step four? I am not rushing you, Gretl?"

"No, you're not. Step four is when the whole team – let's say Paul and all the people who report directly to him, Armand, Brian, and the others – get together to study each other's position descriptions and talk about their responsibilities, authorities, and accountabilities. By the end of step four, Brian tells me, the team knows exactly what they each do and how they fit together, so there are no gaps or overlaps in responsibilities. Do you see how it works?"

"Absolutely. It seems like a lot of work, but it makes a lot of sense. I begin to understand why Armand is so happy these days. Paul has given him a real job to do and he is asking him to get it done without any interference from him. And if Armand makes a mess of things, Paul will have his bottom for a necktie. It seems this should be the end of the exercise. What else can there be to do?"

"First of all, Michelle, it is 'balls, not bottom'. A bit difficult to have a bottom for a necktie."

"But it must also be difficult to have balls for a necktie."

"Well, they hang there, if you know what I mean."

"You want to see Armand's big bottom. It also hangs there, even more than his balls."

They both giggled at the image of Armand's bottom. "It'll be difficult for me not to laugh next time I see Armand and his *derrière*."

"Don't worry about that, *chérie*. He will probably laugh with you if you tell him. Now what about step five?"

"That's probably the most interesting of all the steps. I remind you. At the end of step four, everybody in the team knows what each other's jobs are about. That doesn't mean that there aren't problems. For example, problems with pay, holiday schedules, working conditions, training, literally dozens of things. Then you have problems with other people with whom you do not get on, and so on. If you can imagine any problem at work, they may have it. And having a work-related problem can affect your ability to do your job. Any questions so far?" she asked.

"Not at all. You are doing very well, darling. Brian must be a wonderful teacher."

"Thank you, darling, sarcasm will get you everywhere, so I'll ignore these catty remarks. Step five consists of giving everyone in the team a special questionnaire – OCAT, Brian calls it. It stands for *organizational climate assessment technique*. In that questionnaire, they can show how unhappy they are with something, anything. And then the team sit down and discuss the results. It's incredible what comes out: for example, minor points that Brian never thought about, but which have annoyed one of his team for months, even years. And that person never wanted to talk about it with someone who could make it all right, for any number of reasons. Well, they can now speak about these matters quite freely, and then it's up to the team leader to try and resolve any specific problem, or at least explain why it can't be resolved."

"So that is step five? Armand went through that step with his team last week. He came home shaking his head. He told me he had a list as long as your arm of things he had to fix for his people. But, as he said to me *en passant*, he may not be able to fix all of them, but at least now he knows about these problems."

"That's the important thing about step five, Michelle. A team leader finds out what problems his team members may be having and he can try to do something about them."

"So that is the end of the story. Once you go through this exercise, you are fixed for life."

"Not at all. Once a year they have to go through the process all over again. In this way they make sure that they know if something has changed or needs changing in all the different jobs, or if any of the members of a team has a new problem which requires resolution. Brian thinks it will work very well."

Michelle looked at her watch. "*Mon Dieu!* Britt and Gloria

are late. Gloria maybe, but not our German *fräulein*. That is not like Beebee at all."

Gretl, who was facing the entrance to the dining room, held up her hand and waved. "Speak of the devil, there they are. And not a moment too soon. I'm dying for a drink."

There were kisses all around as they took their places at the table and signalled for a waiter to take their drink order. Michelle, irrepressible as usual, directed her first comment at Britt. "You are looking gorgeous, darling. And that beautiful dress. Prospects must be good for your little company, *non*?"

"Everything is going so well, Ronny ordered me to take the day off, buy myself anything I like, and go and have a long lunch with all of you. I'm sorry I am late, but I could not find anything until I saw this number. I am glad you like it, Michelle. Ronny will like it too, I think." Changing her tone of voice, she looked at the wives of her former colleagues with genuine affection. "It is so good to see you all again. It has been so long."

"We all seem to get carried away with our own little lives," Gloria intoned, nervously turning the pages of her menu. "I'm sorry to be late also, but Tony was in one of his worse than usual moods. I shan't bore you with the details. Let's order instead."

The three friends exchanged significant looks as they realized that they were being especially insensitive. Gloria had apparently had a difficult morning. Nothing more was said as they studied their menus and waited for their drinks to arrive.

It was Gloria who broke the silence. "So, what's the news? How are things at Mobile Auto Warehouses, Beebee? You were saying things are good. Tell us about it."

Britt looked at her other two friends for guidance and received none. "Well, we seem to be going OK, Gloria," she started lamely. "Ron is working hard, and me too . . ."

"Let's get something straight, girls," Gloria interrupted her. "Just because I'm having a lousy time with a husband who's not adapting well to being unemployed doesn't mean we have to walk on eggs around each other. We've been friends far too long for that. He'll find something soon. In the meantime, let's forget about my problems and catch up on the gossip."

Gretl, never one to hesitate, took the initiative. "In that case, I say we ought to place our food order, and then hear what's been happening in the Johns household. This is what concerns us more than anything else."

They gave their orders to the waiter and turned to Gloria, who was shaking her head and half-smiling to herself. "You truly want to know? Well, it's awful. Tony continued going into the consultants every day for the first five or six weeks after he was made redundant, sending out applications, phoning anyone and everyone he thought might know something, thinking laterally with the consultants about other job possibilities. Then he began to miss a day here and there. I have no idea where he went, but he'd come home at night as if he'd been at the consultancy as usual. In the meantime, the consultants would phone to find out where he was and I'd have to pretend I'd given him a bunch of jobs around the house which had had to be done urgently, or he couldn't come to the phone because he was out at the shops for me. And he'd pretend to me that he'd been at the consultancy, and so it went on, the lies flying thick and fast. Now he doesn't pretend any more. He doesn't go in at all. He sits in front of the television and glares at anyone who talks to him. He used to like gardening, doing odd jobs. Now he wouldn't lift a finger if the house fell down around him."

"But that is terrible, Gloria," Michelle couldn't resist exclaiming.

"Are you telling us there hasn't been a single lead, a single job offer in all these months?" Gretl asked.

"Yes. Actually, that's not true. A friend offered him a night watchman's job as a fill in. And Tony would have taken it, except he would have to go through a three-week intensive course to qualify or the insurance wouldn't cover that friend's business premises. Shall I go on? He's just too old at the age of fifty-three. That, together with his reputation in the pharmaceutical industry, effectively bars him from finding any employment where he can use his training, his skills and his experience. Let's face it, the pharmaceutical industry is all he knows. And, at this moment, he's not prepared to try anything new."

There was silence as they struggled to come to terms with the tragedy Gloria was experiencing every day and night. Their food arrived and they started eating.

Britt put her fork down. "Tony must come and work with Ron and me," she declared in her flat matter-of-fact voice. "He will be so much help to us both in so many ways. I do not know why Ron and I did not think about it before. So, this afternoon, Gloria, I talk to Ron and we prepare carefully the things Tony will have to do. And then we come and see Tony, show him what his job will be and how important it is for MAW, we discuss salary and a percentage of the business, and he can start with us next week. And he does not need any stupid training. He already knows too much. That is settled."

There were tears in Gloria's eyes as she looked across the table at Britt. "I know that stems from real friendship, dearest Britt. But you don't know Tony. He's very proud and he won't accept charity. He knows almost as much about your business as you and Ron do. He'll know straight away you can't afford anyone like him in an operation which is just starting out. It was a lovely thought . . ."

"This is not charity, Gloria. We need someone like Tony to keep us from making mistakes," Britt immediately countered.

"But Britt, I know what he'll say. In fact, I think it may make him feel his inadequacies even more. No. Tony is going to have to dig himself out of this one by himself, that's all there is to it. Something will turn up eventually."

"But if he's given up looking for a job any more, how will he ever find one, Gloria?" Gretl asked her.

"He will. He'll get up one morning and start all over again. He did that years ago when we were first married. That's the way he is. Enough of Tony and all our depressing news. Let's talk about something else. How are things at H & H for Armand

and Brian? I hope life is being tough for them too." She tried to grin as she spoke, but the tears were close.

"*Eh bien, ma chère . . .*"

"I'm joking, Michelle and Gretl. I hear it is all going very well for them, and I think that's wonderful."

"Seriously, Gloria, they have never had to work as hard before, even though they say they are enjoying it, surprise, surprise," Gretl quickly cut in. "But I want to know more about MAW, Britt, before we get on to the subject of H & H again. When do you expect to make your tenth million? You and Ron must promise to take us all for a cruising holiday on your big yacht when you do . . ."

Chapter 21

10.30 p.m., Friday, 7 November

Holman B. Andrews helped Mary Ruffin out of her chair. "That was an absolutely splendid dinner, my dear. I can see I'm going to visit my newest division more often. And I promise to bring Louise next time. She enjoyed meeting you so much when you and Paul came to dinner."

They led the procession of seven diners into the lounge where the maid was waiting to pour coffee from a solid silver tray, complete with solid silver coffee urn, milk pitcher and sugar bowl. Paul made his way to the ornate bar at the far end of the large room. It was not exactly his taste in bars, though he never argued with Mary concerning domestic matters. But then the whole pretentious house was not what he would have chosen to live in.

In her inimitable style, Mary had suddenly decided she would rejoin him. In one day, without consulting him, she had rented this outrageously expensive house, complete with sauna, swimming pool and tennis court. Then she had emptied their large penthouse overlooking the river of its antique furniture, including the Louis XVI gilt lounge suite, and hired two men for two days to move that furniture around and hang the two dozen or so original paintings she had acquired over the years. She had not stopped until she was satisfied that her prized possessions were displayed to their best advantage, and in three days, she had succeeded in making it look as if they had lived in the house for the last ten years.

This was their first dinner party, in part to christen their new home, but mostly to impress his boss, on an official visit to the division. He had to give her all due credit. She could turn a simple meal at home into an extravaganza, complete with an appropriately dressed maid and chef, the maid to serve the dinner and pour the wine, the chef to arrange the catered gourmet four-course dinner tastefully on her exquisite Royal Doulton service. Her attention to detail was considerable, which explained why she was such a successful public relations consultant and earned almost as much as he did.

He looked at her across the elegant room as she made small talk with their guests. As usual, she was beautifully turned out in a simple, but very expensive, Paisley chiffon dress, her lustrous dark hair gathered on her head in an attractive bun. He supposed he had been fortunate to have found her, and to have adjusted reasonably well to a childless marriage. She played the part of consort to a senior executive superbly and, in many ways, he attributed much of his rapid rise in H & H to her. As she reminded him from time to time, she had made a huge investment in his career and he must play his part. It was simply not enough to be an outstanding scientist and an excellent manager.

One of the principal tenets of their conjugal arrangement was that there was never to be the slightest hint of scandal to endanger his upward mobility, which explained why he had so suddenly left the Curtis barbecue earlier that year. He would have given his eyeteeth to have made love to Britt Berghoff that afternoon, and he was quite certain that it would have been a memorable experience. But he was also aware that the consequences could have been disastrous. On balance, he felt he had made the right decision, even if he invariably felt a touch of regret whenever he thought about that lost opportunity. And he did every so often, especially when he lay beside Mary in their king-size bed, her back to him.

He took the tray with the six ports and the cognac to Mary and their guests. Armand was the only one who had opted for a brandy liqueur which he proceeded to swirl around in the balloon and occasionally sniff appreciatively. It had always amused Paul to see how different people reacted to brandy in a balloon. Some held the glass to the light to examine the oily tracks on the sides, others smacked their pursed lips as they took tiny sips, still others held the balloon in both hands to warm the contents. But no one, it seemed, ever drank the brandy without some gesture or affectation. It appeared that Armand was no different.

His introspection was interrupted by Mary who proposed the first toast of the evening in faultless French, "*Soyez les bienvenus, mes bons amis*," smiling at Michelle and Armand, Gretl and Brian, but her eyes finally coming to rest on their guest of honour, Holman B. Andrews, who acknowledged her look with an appreciative nod. She was perfectly cast in the role of hostess, even if the show was all on the outside. Paul wondered if she could ever warm sufficiently to someone, man or woman, to enjoy a satisfying sexual relationship. He would have liked her to find some fulfilment, even for a little while, the kind that Michelle Hernier had with her overweight husband whom she so obviously adored, or Gretl Curtis who was obviously so comfortable with Brian. He suspected most people would see the Ruffins as the ideal professional couple, deeply attached to each other, complementing each other in every way. He certainly thought Mary saw their relationship in that light. If she only knew how close he had been to taking that luscious toxicologist to bed and committing the twin unpardonable sins of betraying her trust in him and having an affair with a subordinate. He rose to go to the bar. It was time to replenish glasses. Armand was apparently doing more sniffing than drinking. It would be a while before he needed more brandy.

"I think you should know, Mary, that Paul is doing a magnificent job," Holman Andrews declared unexpectedly, bowing slightly to Paul who was returning from the bar with the port decanter. "And may I add that his choice of lieutenants has been outstanding." Once again he bowed slightly to Brian and Armand. "I can't imagine what it would have been like in Research, Armand, had Carla Nielson taken your position. At the last minute, on some intuition, I encouraged her to go to another company. My latest information is that she's proving to be an absolute disaster as a manager. Mind you, she's a very capable medicinal chemist, but I don't have to tell you that it takes more than being a good scientist to be a good manager as well. So, here's to the three of you and, from what I understand, I can look forward to some positive news from this division quite soon. Let me assure you, all sorts of good things will descend on you and yours if you can put a money-spinner on the market for us by this time next year."

The fact that Holman Andrews had a background in marketing had not escaped the three scientists. Holman's statement illustrated admirably the perennial problem of all pharmaceutical companies: the difference in emphasis between the scientific and the commercial. Armand was quick to react. He put his brandy balloon down on the mahogany coffee table in front of him, crossed his arms across his chest and sat back in his gilt Louis XVI armchair. It creaked ominously under his weight.

Michelle leaned anxiously sideways and touched his knee. "Be careful, *chéri*. Mary will never forgive us if you destroy her beautiful chair."

Brian broke through the muted, rather nervous, laughter. "I'm almost as concerned with what he's going to say. Whenever Armand assumes that pose, it signals he's about to make a profound statement. Be advised, Holman."

"I'm on my guard, Brian. I've been told he's a formidable opponent."

Armand straightened and dropped his arms onto his stomach, a twinkle in his eyes. "*Alors*, there are no secrets from anyone.

I have a reputation, it seems. Then I should not worry about putting my shoe in my mouth."

Gretl giggled. "You put your foot in your mouth, Armand darling, not your shoe."

"Is there a difference, *Madame* smartypants?"

Paul raised his hand to attract Holman and Mary's attention. Mary especially was watching this exchange with increasing concern. "I had better explain. There are four couples who do almost everything together, and have done so for as long as the HE Division has been in existence. At work, they are even known as the three musketeers, with Brian as D'Artagnan. The Herniers and the Curtises, the Johns and a highly talented toxicologist called Britt Berghoff who has apparently had an impressive assortment of boyfriends over the years. Incidentally, Holman, Tony Johns was the director of regulatory affairs in the division and became redundant soon after the takeover. Britt Berghoff resigned in March and went into a spare parts business with her mechanic boyfriend. My understanding is they're making a huge success of their venture."

"What are you trying to say, Paul?" Mary inquired impatiently.

"In a nutshell, Mary, you need to take whatever you observe going on between the Herniers and the Curtises with a sizeable grain of salt."

"I had already gathered something special exists between them," Holman Andrews observed thoughtfully. "The fact remains that Armand was about to make an observation before your explanation. If it doesn't bother you too much, Mary, I'd like to hear what he has to say."

Armand looked quizzically at Holman Andrews for a moment. Brian expected, with trepidation, that Armand would take issue with the company president over the meaning of research. "We finally have some promising drugs in the pipeline, Holman, that is true. Perhaps this time next year we start making some money for H & H, which will please everyone, especially the men and women in this division. But this did not happen by chance alone."

Holman Andrews sensed Armand was intent on getting a special message across. "Tell us more, Armand."

"Nothing would have happened if it had not been for your choice of the division's general manager, Paul Ruffin. Let me say that I disliked him very much to begin with. But he has gained my respect as a very professional manager in all that he does."

With heartfelt relief, Brian registered his agreement with a loud "Hear, hear!".

Paul had gone red with embarrassment, but he quickly tried to turn that vote of confidence into a joke. "I think you should know, Holman, it cost me a large sum to bribe Armand and Brian to tell you that."

Holman Andrews acknowledged Paul with a smile, and nodded, "Of course." He turned back to Armand, the smile gone now, his face grimly determined. "I rarely feel it necessary to defend my position. Nevertheless, let me make this observation. I may be a marketer in charge of a technology-based organization, but I got where I have because I'm a good judge of people, because I've almost always been able to put a square peg into a square hole. I didn't appoint Paul because Mary throws a wonderful dinner party." He turned to her. "In all fairness, it helps enormously for a man to have a clever wife and superb hostess by his side." He turned to Armand once more. "But when the chips are down, a man has to prove himself at the workface, not over dinner and drinks."

Once again Brian registered his agreement with a "Hear, hear!". He addressed Holman Andrews in his quiet voice. "All the same, I think you should know it wasn't easy putting the division together again. Morale was so low as to be practically non-existent after all the sackings and the changes. I have been lucky to work closely with Paul on a very difficult exercise: changing the personnel culture of the organization into a *high involvement workforce*. And we're substantially there, I'm happy to report. Morale has never been higher and commitment to our objectives is total."

Brian smiled across at Paul who was sitting on the edge of his chair, twirling his glass of port. "There were times, however, when I know he could cheerfully have chopped off a few heads and adopted a completely authoritarian approach. But he didn't, and more power to him for that. He sat in the middle of this frustrating void and patiently waited for the right opportunities to put the pieces into place. You've heard him talk about his Advisory Committee and how he couldn't manage properly without it now. Well, it wasn't always like this." Brian turned to Paul. "Tell Holman about it, Paul. It makes a great story."

Paul held up his hand. "If you think it needs telling, Brian, go right ahead. You know what happened as well as, if not better than, me."

"If you wish." He turned to Holman Andrews. "The Advisory Committee meets once a month. For the first five months of its existence, Paul would come into our Communications Committee after each meeting and tell us that nothing had happened. By this I mean that the elected members of the Advisory Committee had told Paul there were no problems anywhere in the division, and they had no suggestions on how to help him solve problems at his level. Each month we would ask him if anything had happened, and each month he would tell us 'Nothing'. Then he would have a little rant and rave about that no-good group of smartarse elected no-hopers who were having a great time making him look like an absolute fool. In turn, we would advise him to have patience – they would come round to his way of thinking in time. After their fifth monthly meeting, he came into our meeting and I thought he was going to have a heart attack, Mary. 'Do you know what problems they've finally told me they have?' he asked us. 'They want the men's lavatory on the second floor painted a soft shade of blue, and they want an extra coffee machine in the smokers' cafeteria. I'll tell you what I'm going to do. I'm going to have the men's lavatory on every floor painted black, and I'm going to close the smokers' cafeteria and tell them they can only smoke outside the building, and I hope their backsides freeze off. And then I'm going to disband the AC and go back to being an authoritarian son of a bitch.'"

"I think I can guess what happened next, Brian. But please continue," Holman interrupted, a broad grin on his face.

"You're right, Holman. We all jumped on him. You should have heard Isabel Esporanta . . ."

"Don't remind me," Paul cut in. "She rarely says anything at meetings. But for a moment there, I thought she was going to cut out my liver. Let me add that the others weren't far behind her, especially you, Brian, as I recall."

"You're perfectly right. If she hadn't gone for you, though, I certainly would've. Anyway, we all told him in no uncertain terms that they were testing him. They wanted to see how genuine he was about fixing any problem that came up from the floor. We told him he had to get these two requests fulfilled, the sooner the better. And he did, that very week. Then the floodgates opened and he's never looked back. Now he rarely makes an important decision concerning the division without first taking it into the AC. He even takes the recommendations of the Operating Committee into the AC, which doesn't make us, his lieutenants, too happy."

"But you can live with that," Paul observed.

"How many committees do you have, Paul?" Holman asked.

"Just the three," Paul replied.

"Which are?" Holman continued.

"The Operating Committee, which consists of my immediate subordinates and other supernumeraries who join us from time to time as expert witnesses. That committee mostly determines policy and research priorities. The Communications Committee deals with human resource matters. And the Advisory Committee, which is elected, is my pipeline to the workforce, and my biggest critic."

Mary interrupted at that moment, an anxious edge to her voice. "I wonder if anyone would like more coffee. Paul, do you think Armand would like some brandy?"

Holman Andrews immediately stood. "Mary, Michelle, Gretl,

I apologize. We tend to forget that sometimes there are certain occasions when work should not dominate the conversation."

"Not at all, Holman," Gretl spoke up. "I've found this absolutely fascinating. Brian rarely comes home and tells me about these situations."

"Just as well," Paul observed, doing the rounds with the port decanter and the brandy bottle, as everyone laughed.

"Yes," Mary commented lamely, at a loss for words. Brian could not remember when he had last seen her not in total control of her own dinner party. Maybe Holman and the others were going to be good for her. Maybe a little more of the softening influence of Gretl and Michelle, and she might not present her back to him so often in bed. There was a time, early in their marriage, when things had been so good between them. He was brought back to reality. "Paul, darling, could I have some more port?" she asked him sweetly, almost tenderly, a warm light in her eyes.

Chapter 22

3.50 p.m., Thursday, 11 December

Ingrid Andersen clipped a large diagram of *the change model* on the easel. Then, on the cork board which ran the length of one wall of the large room, she pinned another model illustrating an *effective human organization* being supported by three columns interconnected by arrows. Next to it, she also pinned the explanations for these three columns:

1. *Good personnel practices* If employees are to have jobs which satisfy their individual and unique needs, there must be *informed human resource expertise* to advise and assist line management to engage in a wide range of activities designed to enhance employees' perceptions of their current jobs and their long-term prospects in the enterprises that employ them.
2. *Good participation mechanisms* If employees are to have *a real say in decisions* that are likely to affect them, there must be appropriate mechanisms by which they are kept informed about events as these occur, and they must be trained to participate on

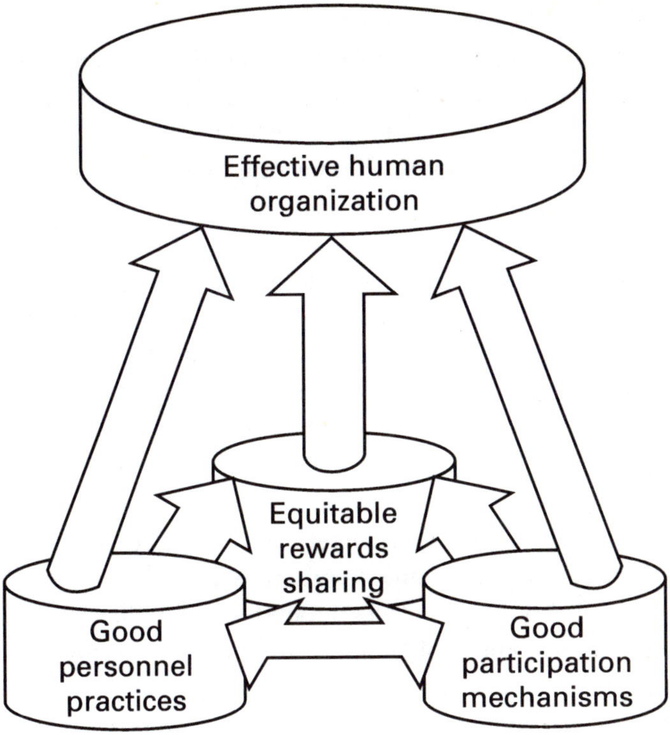

Effective human organization

equitable terms in the decision-making processes of the enterprises that employ them.

3. *Equitable rewards sharing* If employees are to share in the profits they help generate, there must be *an equitable reward sharing system* which recognizes, in an immediate and tangible way, the contributions they make to the financial success of the enterprises that employ them.

Satisfied with the visual displays, she glanced quickly around the new headquarters of the divisional Human Resource Department, to satisfy herself everything was in place. After all, she was about to have the first formal meeting in her office cum training centre, library, equipment and storage room. Some months before, soon after she had assumed the mantle of HR manager, Paul Ruffin had instructed her in an offhand manner to go ahead and get whatever she needed to do her job, and she had. He would be chairing the meeting of the Advisory Committee and would have his first look at her little empire.

She was proud of what she had achieved. The HR Centre was a former locker room, with *en suite* shower and toilet facilities, in the basement next to the grossly underutilized gymnasium. Everything in that large square room had come from other areas of the building. Her desk and chair had come from the third floor and had once been used by Security as they monitored people entering and leaving the research laboratories. The wooden table and twelve chairs, sitting in the middle of the room, had come from the cafeteria on the ground floor. The bookcases had mostly come from Brian Curtis's former office, and a couple of other places around the building. She had returned on a number of Sundays and painted the green walls and the ten steel lockers white, converting these into storage cupboards. The long stainless steel table in the corner had come from Development on the fifth floor. It had once been used for dissecting animals and, somewhere along the way, had fallen over, a welding coming apart. This had apparently made it unusable for the sterile environment of the laboratory. It was now covered with a crisp white plastic tablecloth on which she had placed the electric coffee maker, cups and saucers, and an outsize glass container full of shortbread. The door, now bearing an enamel plaque with *Human Resource Department* in scrolled letters, opened to face a wall covered with colourful motivational posters.

She looked for a final time at the ten sets of pads and pencils to make sure they were neatly arranged around the table, and the dozen glasses and two water carafes were attractively grouped in the middle. She hoped that these little touches, as well as the smell of coffee and the bright posters, would encourage people to drop by and talk about organizational and personal matters, as well as enhance the significance of her department.

There was a quiet knock on the open door. Colin Gillespie and Shirley McLeod from Administration peered in. "Are we in the right place, Mrs Andersen?" Shirley asked hesitantly.

Ingrid advanced quickly towards them. "My name is Ingrid. It has not changed since the last time we met, Shirley. This is where the Advisory Committee will meet from now on." She led them in and waited as they looked around. "This is the first meeting in this room, so you will have to be kind and say you like it, please."

Colin Gillespie, a senior accountant, shook his head. "Wasn't this a locker room?"

"Just so," Ingrid replied.

"I love it, Ingrid. What a great job," Shirley exclaimed.

"It's certainly a remarkable transformation. Did you raid an upmarket second-hand shop for all this furniture and equipment," Colin asked, a half-smile on his serious face.

"I did not spend a penny," she informed them solemnly. "It was all lying around the building, not being used."

Unerringly, Colin went to the stainless steel corner table and lifted the plastic sheet to expose the top. "Do you know what this table would have cost when we first bought it, Ingrid? Thousands. I used to process the invoices."

"Goodness," she exclaimed. "They did not want it. They had a stock of old telephone directories on it. You think I should take it back?"

They were interrupted as the other members of the committee arrived and looked around. There was general agreement that she had done a wonderful job with the cast-offs she had obtained. However, what was also needed was a lounge suite and coffee table to entertain her visitors in comfort.

Reg McGee, an animal handler and cleaner from Development, looked at his watch. He raised his hand to attract the attention of the ten people standing by the corner table, helping themselves to coffee and shortbread. "Guess what, folks, our fearless leader is late for the first time."

"No, I'm not, Reg. Your watch is thirty seconds fast," Paul Ruffin called out as he stood at the door and looked around. They responded to that unexpected announcement with laughter and good-natured gibes directed at Reg. Paul continued standing at the door for a full minute, taking everything in. "So this is where the boardroom coffee urn finished up," indicating the electric coffee maker with an accusing forefinger. "No wonder you never gave me any invoices to approve. You've been on a pilfering spree around the building." Once again, there was laughter as the members of the committee reacted positively to his humour. "Well, let me tell you, Ingrid, it looks a lot better here than where you found these bits and pieces. I think this is great. Well done. All the same, I think you're taking our projected profit-sharing scheme a little too seriously." Without another word, he advanced to the table. "Where would you like us to sit, madam secretary, and who's going to offer me a cup of coffee from my own coffee maker?"

They quickly seated themselves in their designated places and opened their folders, taking their coffee cups and shortbread to the table.

"This is the seventh meeting of the Advisory Committee, ladies and gentlemen," Paul intoned, opening the meeting. "It is also the last of our meetings for the year. I want to break with the usual procedure and launch directly into a review of the change programme." There was a shuffling of feet and movement in chairs as they considered his proposal. "I'll allow some time at the end if there's anything that can't wait until our next meeting in January. Any comments or objections?" He waited the statutory ten seconds. There were none.

"Very well. Let's proceed. First, I've now heard back from head office about our proposal on profit sharing. They are prepared to try it for a period of two years, starting from the beginning of next year. At the end of that time, it will be reviewed by the corporation board. Net profit for the division will be distributed as follows. Investment in divisional growth will be determined by a joint committee of divisional personnel and head office, based on divisional and corporate needs. This charge on net profit must be made before anything else is determined. Next, to satisfy shareholder requirements, they want the prime lending rate plus 4 per cent. What is left after that is to be divided equally between the company and the employees. They feel strongly that the employee portion should be distributed in a way that reflects the contribution of individual members of the division to that profit. That's it in a nutshell." Paul leaned back in his chair. "Over to you."

By common agreement, eyes turned to Colin Gillespie. He had been largely responsible for the proposal and they deferred to him for comment. "Let me make sure I have it right, Paul. The instructor on the training course Ingrid arranged for us to attend called it *feedback*. After net profit is struck, that amount will be divided into three parts. The first bite at the cherry will be to ensure that divisional needs for the coming twelve months are satisfied. I'm talking about research and development projects, new equipment, in fact, all the bits and pieces that generate growth. The next bite will be to ensure that shareholders obtain a fair return on their investment. They propose this should be prime lending rate, whatever that is at the time, plus 4 per cent. The last bite, what's left, is to be divided equally between the corporation and the employees, the corporation's 50 per cent to go into consolidated revenue, the remaining 50 per cent to be distributed among the employees. This is essentially what we proposed some three months ago. Have I got it right?"

Paul did not hesitate. "Spot on, Colin."

"As to the method for distributing our 50 per cent, we suggested this be divided equally between all employees," Colin continued. "Head office now think that we should have some method for rewarding employees differentially, presumably based on each employee's assumed contribution to profitability. We've been through that before. We don't feel that's at all fair.

Employees are already paid a salary which reflects their individual potential impact on organizational profits. I don't have to tell you that some scientists are paid four, five times more than most employees. If we are forced to adopt the head office proposal, it will be considered by everyone in the division to be a form of double-dipping, which will make the profit-sharing scheme far less attractive. How adamant is head office on that issue?"

Paul shrugged. "They urge us strongly to see it their way. I suspect they see our profit-sharing scheme as something that may catch on. If it does, they don't want to establish a precedent where senior executives, who make the important, the money-generating, decisions, are not rewarded accordingly. It opens up a floodgate of potential problems down the road. It's probably also a form of egalitarianism they are having difficulty accepting."

There was a moment of silence as everyone around the table considered the implications of the head office counter-proposal.

Matthew Abbot, a young Ph.D. chemist from Research, raised his hand. "I don't think we can allow them to determine that aspect of the profit-sharing arrangement. It *is* a powerful demonstration of egalitarianism. What we're saying by proposing an equal split between *all* employees is that we *all* contribute to profits, but in different ways. We have no trouble acknowledging that market forces dictate salaries and wages. But we also have to acknowledge that money is made not only from good ideas, but also from not spending it. Hell, Paul, just look round this room. If Ingrid had taken you at your word, she could have spent three or four thousand dollars fitting out this room, a lot more if she began knocking down walls and who knows what else. By foraging around the building and making do – superbly, by the way – she's increased the division's profit by that amount. That's what we're talking about, and that's what they have to understand at head office if profit sharing is to be the glue that binds together all the other proposals we've been implementing." He waved his hand in the general direction of the models on the easel and the cork board.

"Ingrid, make a note of the glue business. I'm going to need this metaphor if I'm to convince head office we're not a bunch of raving anarchists. Leave this with me, team. I think I can convince head office that the equal distribution proposal has the support of everyone in the division, especially me, and they have to give it a try, whatever their misgivings." He pointed at the two models. "Now let's concentrate on what we've achieved, and what is still left to do. Ingrid, fire away," and he pushed his chair away from the table and faced the models.

Ingrid went to *the change model* on the easel.[1] She pointed at *leadership*. "I do not know if this is the best place to begin, but I think it is not possible to teach people to be leaders. I am also not sure it is possible to ask someone to fill in a questionnaire and tell if that person is a leader. I am suspicious when someone tells me he can do these things with success. I think we waste money when we pay consultants to do these things. I think we get better value for our time and our money with the five-stage *team development exercise*. We must ask ourselves, 'Do we want to turn all our people into leaders, even if we could do that, or do we want to have people working better as a team, with any member of the team becoming a leader when it is necessary?' I am a bit with Fred Fiedler and his *contingency leadership*[2] on this one. That is how I feel." She stood by the easel and waited.

Deslee Watson from Development, a senior veterinary pathologist, raised her hand. "I've been through both experiences: *leadership training* and the *team development exercise*. I'm inclined to agree with Ingrid. I thought it was good to have an expert explain what there was to know about leadership. I doubt, though, whether it made me more effective as a leader. Was it worth the money to send me to that workshop? It depends. I personally found it very interesting, even enjoyable, a pleasant break from work. However, I don't think it's going to make me

1 See page 180
2 Fiedler, F.E., Chemers, M.M. and Maher, L. (1976), *Improving Leadership Effectiveness: The Leader Match Concept*, New York: John Wiley.

a better supervisor, which means that the money was largely wasted. But there's no doubt in my mind about the effectiveness of the *team development exercise*. It opened my eyes to many steps I should be taking both with and for my team, and I'm busy working on that aspect right now. I also know that the exercise will pay off handsomely in the short and in the long term."

Reg McGee interrupted. "Does this mean we ought to save money and not send people on these courses?"

Ingrid quickly cut in. "We must be careful not to throw out the baby with the bath before we make a decision . . ." She was interrupted when everyone started laughing, much to her consternation.

Shirley McLeod raised her voice to make herself heard. "You don't throw out the bath with the baby, just the bath *water*."

Paul interrupted, anxious to maintain the concentration of the meeting. "I think I hear Ingrid and some of you saying that we must be much more careful how we spend our training dollars. This is a matter for Human Resource to determine and advise. I don't think we should spend any more time on this. Let's keep moving."

Ingrid pointed at the next factor on the model, *human resource function*. "I only want to say you now have a Human Resource manager, and also a Human Resource Centre. I hope you will be patient with me. I am still learning how to be a good Human Resource manager."

Colin Gillespie raised his hand. "I'm not sure this is the best time to raise the subject, everyone, but I think Ingrid is doing a fabulous job. I also think we should ask the division general manager to consider purchasing a lounge suite and a coffee table for this HR Centre. I don't mean anything expensive. In fact, I know where there are some real bargains. It means less in the profit kitty, but what the hell! She's earned it."

There was enthusiastic agreement around the table.

Paul smiled at Ingrid who was standing by the easel blushing furiously. "Done. Colin, arrange with Ingrid when and where you take her shopping. You should know how to get the invoice paid. If anyone questions this expenditure, send them to me. Now, back to you, Ingrid. Let's keep moving."

Reg McGee half raised his hand. They all recognized the sign. Behind that seemingly naïve expression, there lurked a mind that was as sharp as a razor. "I don't know whether this is at all important . . ."

Colin Gillespie interrupted. "Get on with it, Reg."

"Well, we have another drawing . . ."

Colin Gillespie interrupted again. "Model, Reggie."

"Yes, model. I want Ingrid to tell us more about it, especially the circle with *good personnel practices*."

There was a moment of silence as everyone reread the legend. Paul was the first to react. "Well, madam manager of Human Resource? That's a fair question."

"It is what it says. I am here to help you."

Reg persisted. "How are you helping us?"

"Well, Personnel or Human Resource management does all kinds of things for employees. For example, people leave and we have to replace them. This is called *recruitment, selection and induction*. Human Resource finds people who want the job, helps select the best one and inducts that person in the way we work, except now all this is done by a small team from the group with whom that person will work. I am only a consultant to this team. Of course, none of this happens unless the group proves they must replace that person. Don't forget, putting more people on the payroll is expensive. Everyone is under pressure to keep costs down so we increase profit because half of that profit belongs to us."

Like Paul, she waited ten seconds before continuing. "Then there is *training for skills and personal development*. For example, all of you have been trained on how to work on a committee. All of you get paid regularly. It is called *salary administration*. We have to organize your holidays so that there is little disruption to the work, we have to arrange your retirement benefits, and so on. Then there are special projects like the *team development exercise*, visits to other plants in the corporation so you know what else is going on and where we fit in . . ."

Paul held up his hand. "The list is almost endless, Reg. HR deals with anything and everything that concerns the morale and wellbeing of people. As an aside, let me add that these activities are always changing. This doesn't mean that Human Resource acts without first consulting, without making sure that what needs to be done makes sense to different people like you, me, and many others around the division. Anyway, that's what it's all about, Reg. Anything else, anyone?" As always, he waited for a few seconds, looking round the table.

Ernie Gable, a maintenance technician from Research, coughed to attract attention. He rarely said anything. "I was thinking. If we had wanted to buy a lounge suite when we were working for AgriBus, how long would it have taken to get approval?"

Shirley McLeod shot back without hesitation. "Forever, if ever."

"Well done, Ernie," Paul exclaimed. "An excellent example of a *high involvement workforce* in action. Over to you once again, Ingrid."

She pointed at *profit sharing*. "This is still in the air, but I know Mr Ruffin will resolve it for the beginning of next year. Not that I think it will stay that way. Some of us think it is not right that there should be a profit distribution only once a year. We would like to see a profit distribution at the end of every week, even every day. It is important to reward people as quickly as possible for trying as hard as they can. It is called *positive feedback*, except that we know it will be difficult to make it work. But we must find some way of distributing profits at least every three months."

Paul was shaking his head from side to side as the implications of her statement sank in. "I think Ingrid is giving us notice of motion that she is only just beginning to warm up to her job. Well, team, it sounds as if next year is going to be interesting."

"You haven't heard it all, chief," Colin Gillespie said quietly.

"Ingrid and I and a few others have been looking at *share ownership*. There are all sorts of possibilities, good for H & H and good for us. I suppose what Ingrid and I are saying is that *equitable reward sharing* is a much bigger subject than the profit-sharing scheme we currently have on the table," waving at the model on the cork board.

Paul sank into his chair, showing that he was beginning to feel overwhelmed. "Let's leave a few things for next year, Colin."

Taking the cue from Paul, Ingrid started again. "Next we have *delegation of responsibilities and authorities* and *cohesive small groups*. I think they are part of the *team development exercise*."

"I agree," Paul said. "I also think *information sharing processes* and *employee participation* hang together. This committee is a good example."

Once again Reg McGee raised his hand. "Are we included in *good participation mechanisms*?" he asked, indicating the model on the cork board.

"Absolutely," Paul replied. "What do you think, Ingrid?"

"I agree, Dr Ruffin. And so are the regular meetings all of you have with the people who elected you to this committee. And the meetings managers and supervisors have with their subordinates. It may sound like lots of meetings, but you must share information and you must let everyone participate in decisions because, if they do not, certainly they are unlikely to support the decision. For example, let's take the Christmas party. It was decided that we should not have it any more. It is an expensive affair, it now has to be paid out of our profits, not by AgriBus, and most prefer to celebrate the end of the year with just a few good friends somewhere else. If you, Dr Ruffin, had decided this on your own, everyone in the division would have been very unhappy, I bet you."

Paul looked around the table to get some impression of their feelings on the subject. "This is news to me. I thought the Christmas party was so deeply entrenched, everyone wanted to have it. How general was agreement on this matter?"

Once again Colin Gillespie spoke out on behalf of the

committee. "We were going to raise the matter with you at the end of the meeting, Paul. Agreement was almost unanimous. Many said they had never enjoyed the party because they couldn't drink and drive. A few even suggested they would much rather line up and receive a bonus cheque from you and spend it with their family and friends. With rare exceptions that's the way it went."

Paul immediately responded. "If that's what everyone wants, that's fine by me. I have to admit, I'm disappointed I won't be able to do the rounds and kiss you ladies a happy Christmas . . ."

Inez Morreno, a laboratory technician from Research, held up her hand. "That is easy, Señor Paul. I will organize the ladies in a line so you can kiss them Merry Christmas. And I will be *numero uno*. Maybe, after you kiss me, you will not want to kiss the others, *non*?"

Amid the general laughter, Arthur Green, one of the gardeners, a good-looking young man, interjected. "Hey! Inez. Maybe I could stand behind the boss and kiss the rest of the girls if he can't get past you."

Paul banged on the table a few times. "Order, gang, order. The meeting has taken a dangerous turn for the better. Back to work. Ingrid, what's left?"

"Only *job security* and *guiding concepts and shared values*."

Paul stood and took a turn about the room, watched by everyone around the table as they recognized the unmistakable signs of tension. He came to a standstill behind his chair. "As long as I'm in the divisional chair, and the bottom doesn't completely fall out of our business, you know you have job security."

"What happens if you leave?" Matthew Abbot immediately countered.

Paul hesitated. "I wish I could give you an unconditional guarantee that everybody has a job for as long as they want it. But a new general manager may want to make changes. I think that person would be foolish to tamper with the *high involvement workforce* we'll have created. These things happen, however, although I hate to admit it."

"What happens if the bottom falls out of our business?" Deslee Watson asked.

"I'd like to think we'll institute a variety of programmes to keep people employed. Job sharing, a shorter workweek, whatever we can do to ensure that some money is going into every home until our prospects improve. In the meantime, it doesn't help to conjecture. You have job security for the foreseeable future," he said with finality and sat heavily in his chair once again. "It is enshrined in our divisional *guiding concepts and shared values*, as you all know. It is also prominent in the corporation's *mission statement*." He turned to Ingrid. "What else is left for discussion? I think we've covered all the issues in *the change model*, and compared and contrasted it with the model that shows what it takes to create an *effective human organization*. Is there anything we haven't done which needed doing by the end of the year?" He looked expectantly around the table. "The bottom line. Do we have the beginnings of a *high involvement workforce*?"

There was a long silence finally broken by Inez Morreno. "Señor Paul, when Sunday night comes, I say to my beautiful Juan, 'Whoopee! Tomorrow it is Monday. I go back to work'. Is this *high involvement workforce*? When I come to work, I like it because there is a good feeling everywhere. Everybody is working hard but also having fun, you know what I mean? We care about what we do and we do the best job we can. Is this *high involvement workforce*? When we see someone else not doing a good job, or making a mistake, we go to that person and we help them do the job right, and they are happy for the help. Is this *high involvement workforce*? What do you think, Señor Paul?"

Colin Gillespie nodded vigorously. "On the button, Inez. I think we have more than the beginnings of a *high involvement workforce*. I think we've become a 'whoopee workforce'. The problem, I think, Paul, is that it's going to take a great deal of work by everyone in the division to keep us there, not just you and Ingrid. Anyway, speaking for myself, the way things stand, I wouldn't want to work anywhere else. If that doesn't make me a member of a *high involvement workforce*, I don't know what does."

Paul looked at Ingrid. "You want to add anything?"

She smiled happily and shrugged as if to say, "What more can I add."

"Is there anything else we should discuss?" He waited the ten seconds. "In that case, let's call it quits. No Christmas party, Inez, but I look forward to your Christmas kiss. Arthur, find some mistletoe and hang it over the front door of the building. You can help me with the kissing – not too much, mind you." And he adjourned the last meeting of the Advisory Committee for the year.

Chapter 23

9.30 a.m., Sunday, 28 December

Armand shifted uneasily in his chair and looked at the other seven people seated around the table drinking coffee, chatting to each other, pretending nothing special was about to happen. It was quite dark in the room, the sky overcast, a brisk westerly blowing, the sea forbidding as the waves crashed thunderously on the beach. He had been delegated the task of presenting their farewell present to Gloria and Tony Johns, with an appropriate little speech. He didn't relish the task one little bit. It would require finesse, of which everyone seemed to think he had an abundance. Well, they would soon find out he was not particularly gifted in that department when everyone began to shed tears. Crying was something they had told him they wanted to avoid at all costs in the final moments before the Johns left the beach house to return to their packing. "You must make with the jokes, darling," Beebee had instructed him, waving her manicured forefinger under his nose. "Absolutely," Gretl had agreed emphatically. "Our farewell present is full of joy, not sadness, and it must evoke happy thoughts."

He drank the remainder of his second cup of coffee, reached

down beside his chair and retrieved the brown paper-covered parcel. It was clearly a framed picture of some kind, not large, but big enough to give him trouble standing it on his stomach and still being able to see over the top. There was an immediate hush, Tony's brow contracting in perplexity, Gloria's eyes opening wide with curiosity. "Gloria and Tony, this is for you. It is our little present to wish you the best of luck for the future. It is our way, even if you will not see us as often in the coming year, to remind you of the wonderful times we have shared with you all these years. It is a French '*à bientôt*' and not an English 'goodbye'. We will see you next year here, at the beach house, and every year after that. And now let me tell you a very funny joke . . ."

Brian held up his hand. "Too late, Armand. The girls are crying. You mucked it up. You should have . . ."

"*Eh, zut alors*, I told you I was not the one to make speeches."

"It doesn't matter now, Armand," Ron quickly cut in, holding a sniffling Britt in his arms. "Just give Gloria and Tony the present."

"*C'est emmerdent, ça.*" He threw his hands up in the air in frustration. "Ladies – especially you, Michelle – enough of this crying. There is nothing to cry about. Tony has found a good job. Yes, they have to leave us because the job is elsewhere. We shall miss them very much. But we should all be so happy for them. It is the beginning of a great adventure and we know they will make of it a huge success. So we have this very special present for you, so you remember well the good friends you leave behind. And here it is. It comes with our love." He handed the parcel to Gloria who was drying her eyes and putting a brave face on the proceedings.

With Tony sitting beside her, Gloria carefully unwrapped the parcel. "How beautiful, Tony," she exclaimed with excitement. "It's a painting of this beach house."

There was a muffled groan from Tony. He stood too quickly, his chair falling over backwards. Not bothering to pick it up, he made a dash for their bedroom and slammed the door behind him. They heard him sobbing, and that affected them all.

"This is the most terrible moment in my life," Armand declared, big tears coursing down his jowls, blowing his nose loudly into his handkerchief.

"Well," Michelle accused him, "it is all your fault, *crétin*." And she put her head on Brian's shoulder.

"It's not his fault at all, Michelle." Gloria put the painting on Tony's overturned chair and walked round the table. She put her arms about Armand and gave him a big hug. "That was the most beautiful speech I've ever heard, which is why Tony was so touched. You are our true friends, all of you. Now I'd better go to Tony. He'll be all right in a moment. It's just been a bad time for him and he couldn't deal with this, on top of everything else." She went through their bedroom door and shut it softly behind her.

Gretl stood. "I don't know about the rest of you, but I need a drink."

"At this hour of the morning?" Brian asked horrified.

"Yes," she told him simply but firmly. "Anyone for a glass of champagne? We were going to open it anyway just before they left. Why not now. We still have another bottle left. Am I right, Ron?"

"I'm sure of it," he replied. "I think it's a great idea. I'll get the bottle, you get the glasses, Gretl."

As they poured champagne, Gloria and Tony quietly rejoined them, Tony looking especially sheepish. Ron immediately handed them each a glass of champagne.

"Brian thinks it's too early in the morning," Beebee informed them, her nose in the champagne glass. "Brian is a stick-in-the-mud and I do not know how Gretl continues to love him. I think she is wasted on him. When was the last time you made love to her in the middle of the morning, darling? Answer that, please."

"None of your business, Beebee," Brian replied. "But since the champagne is out, let's have a toast." He raised his glass.

"To the Johns. Long may they be happy together. Long may they enjoy looking at the painting of this house – actually quite a good piece of work by Coleen something or other. Long may it bring back happy memories of the wonderful holidays we've all spent in it. Finally, here's to the musketeers. All for one and one for all."

They raised their glasses and drank

"You see, Beebee, Brian should have made this speech," Armand informed her. "There would have been no tears and everyone would be very happy."

"I think your little speech was better than Brian's, even if it did make me cry all over Ron's shirt. I think it is time for Tony and Gloria to make a little return speech, do you not think?" she asked, looking at the faces around her.

"I'm not good at making speeches, dear friends," Tony proclaimed lamely.

"A likely excuse from one of the most articulate lawyers I've ever known," Brian interjected.

"As it happens, Brian, I haven't had much practice at making speeches on behalf of my wife and me. The last one I made was when Gloria and I were married. Anyway, let me say how greatly we're going to treasure this painting of our beach house. It will hang over the fireplace in our new home and we expect all of you to visit and see it in its pride of place. Once more, here's to the musketeers." He emptied his glass and placed it carefully on the table upside down. "As you know, I don't have much of a head for champagne at this time of the morning – at any time for that matter. I think Gloria and I should leave before I get drunk or I start crying again."

"*Mais, non,*" Armand exclaimed jokingly. "Not drunk please. I think I like you better crying. Now let me tell you the joke I had for you before you break out into tears . . ."

"This time next year, Athos," Tony interrupted. "I think we'd better go."

Armand gave Tony one of his searching looks. "You are quite

right, Aramis. It is, after all, a not so good joke. But it was only an excuse to keep you with us a little longer."

Beebee put her glass down in mock protest. "D'Artagnan, I still do not want to be Porthos. Just because I have a sexy bottom and good tits does not make me big and fat like him."

For the first time that morning, Tony smiled his crooked smile. He took Britt in his arms and gave her a crushing hug. "There's no doubt about you, my good friends. It's been one hell of a ride all these years." Without saying another word, his head down so they would not see his anguished face, he picked up the painting and headed for the front door, Gloria in tow.

They all trooped out after them in silence and made the rounds of hugs and kisses. Then Tony and Gloria got into his old Toyota and drove slowly away, their hands waving goodbye as they disappeared over the rise.

"I think we should open the second bottle of champagne, and hang the consequences, Brian," Gretl announced as they turned to go back into the house and away from the threatening rain clouds.

"I agree," he informed her unexpectedly. "This is a good day for sitting around and drinking. Come on, Ron, let's see if we can get the girls sloshed enough to want to get back into bed."

"I never have that problem, Brian, sober or sloshed," Ron replied. "With Beebee, it's a matter of conserving my strength for any time of the day or the night."

"*Toujours le grand boaster*, our Ron," Armand called out after him.

Brian popped the cork on the last of the champagne bottles and poured. The girls went into the kitchen with their drinks to prepare hors d'oeuvres. The men sat around the table once again.

"It's been one hell of a year," Brian said to no one in particular, looking out into the gathering storm.

"But especially hard on Gloria, I think," Ron suggested.

"And Tony?" Armand asked. "Do you think it was easy for him?"

Ron thoughtfully turned the fluted glass on the palm of his hand. "I think it was hard on Tony, Armand. But I think it was much harder on Gloria. There was nothing she could do except watch him go down, then up, then down again, for months, until the job appeared out of nowhere."

There was a moment of silence as they recalled how ecstatic they had all been about Tony's job, and astounded when, quite by chance, Brian had found out that Paul Ruffin had arranged it. Tony still didn't know that Paul was behind it, and hopefully Paul would remain unaware that they knew about his part in the matter. And that's the way it should stay, for it would serve no good purpose for Tony or Paul to know.

"He's a funny fellow, Paul Ruffin," Ron declared. "Even yesterday, when he was talking to Tony around the barbecue, he made it seem as if he knew nothing about the business. Do you think, Brian, that the information you have could be wrong and Paul had nothing to do with it after all?"

Brian shook his head. "No way, Ron. I told you, he engineered the whole thing. Albright Cameron have a specialist department which deals exclusively with the pharmaceutical industry. H & H have been associated with them for a long time. As you know, H & H are paranoid about being sued, and I have it on the best authority that after their own lawyers finish their work on the launch of a new product, they send everything to Albright Cameron to make doubly certain that it's all right before it goes to the regulatory authorities and out to the public." He stopped to take a sip of his champagne.

"When Tony phoned to tell me they had approached him, about joining the firm, he asked if I'd be a referee. I know Archie Cameron quite well, so I phoned him to make sure I made all the right points in the reference. He told me it didn't matter what I said; the deal was already done. Paul had apparently gone in to bat for Tony, which was all the recommendation they needed. When I pressed him for more information, it turned out that Paul had alerted them to Tony's availability and had told them he was one of the best legal experts around. In fact, according to Archie, Paul stressed that they would be making a big mistake not to snap him up. So they made Tony an offer, and you know the rest."

"I tell you," Ron replied, "Paul acted yesterday as if everything Tony said about the job was all news to him. I was there, pouring them drinks, while they were discussing the job and working on the barbecue. You know, it's strange, but I never liked him – Paul, I mean. I still have trouble warming to him. He's a cold fish, that one. What do you think, Armand?"

"These are my sentiments exactly, Ron," Armand agreed. "What do you say, Brian. You know him from long before, *non*?"

"I agree. He was just the same at university, single-minded and opportunistic. If he felt someone else had a better idea, he would have no hesitation discarding his own. If he felt he could make capital out of a situation, he would manipulate it to his advantage. For example, let's go back to Tony's job. I wouldn't be surprised if he knows we know. He realized when he was organizing it, that it would cause problems if he told Tony or anyone else, but he'd also have recognized that it would do his own reputation no harm if someone eventually found out. Which is what happened. That's what he's like. We don't have to admire his devious mind. All that should concern us is that he's doing one hell of a great job as division general manager, and he's a damn good boss."

"I don't know what he's doing exactly, Brian, but I think it must be a tough job. I have enough trouble managing one bright spark like Beebee. Imagine having dozens of them all over the place, all of them like you two," Ron observed with a laugh.

"Very funny. Just to be serious for a moment, Ron, it's been tough on everyone. I never told you, Armand, but towards the end of February, I was convinced H & H were going to get rid of everyone and start again with a whole new workforce."

"Isn't putting together a new team of people very expensive?" Ron asked, intrigued by the statement.

"It depends how big the us-and-them problem is likely to be, Ron. When you have a situation where you have to get rid of well over half the employees of the takeover company, and then bring in a large number of new people with different skills, it can be more economical in the long run to start with a clean slate than to try and get them to work together. Fortunately for those of us who are still there, that didn't happen, for there's no doubt in my mind: we're much better off working for H & H than we ever were for AgriBus."

"Why," Ron asked quickly.

"Because AgriBus is not in the human ethicals business," Armand cut in. "All they understand is animals, not people. Fifteen years ago, they make too much money and they have a tax problem. They think if they spend a large slice of that profit on human ethicals research, they get rid of their tax problem, and they make better use of their scientists because there is some synergy between the two kinds of research. There is the chance that if they strike it lucky in one area, they can make it work in the other. After all, Ron, animals are almost like people, *non?*"

"Well, aren't they?"

"No, they are not when you do research," Armand informed him. "Anyway, AgriBus stick with us for fifteen years, through good times and bad. We have lovely jobs then because they do not understand what we do. So we do what we want, which is not much. And we get away with it. It is, like Paul says, a cosy club. Except that the veterinarians are paying the bill. Then one day the directors look at the books and discover we are costing them a fortune, and not getting somewhere fast."

"So you come to work one morning, and you find a big marquee on the lawn," said Ron.

"Right first time, young man," Brian replied, taking over from Armand. "Then the new boys send in Paul Ruffin. They give him the job of making a lean and mean machine. The blood begins to flow. Naturally, they also want results. But blood and results don't go well together. Paul knows he won't get results unless he can get all these different people – many of them angry, all of them hungry – running in the same direction. So he aims for the pot of gold and begins to put together a *high involvement workforce*, which will love the company and do wonderful things. Let's keep things straight. He doesn't do this because he wants to make people happy and productive. He does it because it's just plain good business. How else can you get people running in the same direction unless you line them up on an even playing field, explain the rules, show them what's in it for them and how they can win. Certainly it's also hard work, and offering plenty of opportunities to fall flat on your face – and Paul has had his fair share of that, let me tell you. But he's clung doggedly to his policy because he knows that, once you start a change programme, there's no way to quit without leaving one hell of a mess behind. Moreover, he's going to have to work hard at it all the time from now onwards because if he ever lets up, it'll all come tumbling down like Humpty Dumpty, in little pieces."

Ron thought quietly for a moment as Brian and Armand continued to look out at the pouring rain, then asked reflectively, "Do you think Beebee should have stayed in AgriBus?"

"Who knows," Brian replied. "It doesn't matter now. You're both heavily involved now in your own project, like Paul is with the business of putting together a *high involvement workforce*. And let's face it," he continued, turning to face Ron, "Beebee's rather like Paul. She prefers to organize matters so that she comes out on top. She's going to make you a millionaire, so stick with her."

"You bet, Brian, like a limpet. And, let me tell you, I'm enjoying every moment of the attachment!" Ron exclaimed with a lascivious grin. Brian and Armand both laughed.

"Tell you what, Ronny?" Britt inquired as the girls came out of the kitchen. "From the dirty look on your face, I think you've been talking about me behind my back. And I adore it. So I bring you a plate full of delicious hors d'oeuvres made by the loving hands of your ladies." Britt placed the large plate in the middle of the table. "Since there is no more champagne, you can bring us some wine and be quick about it, Ronny darling. Making hors d'oeuvres is thirsty work."

"See what I mean?" Brian told him with a knowing wink.

And the six friends spread themselves around the table, filled their glasses, and attacked the plate of food. They were, after all, still on holiday, with a few more days to go before they would turn their backs for ever on a very painful year. Not that it mattered any more. They knew now that next year would be very different – and a great deal better.

Commentary

Part I Rumours

Part I sets the stage for the impending takeover. It draws the reader's attention to the range of possible approaches new owners may take to a takeover, and their consequences. It also provides a sample of the reactions employees may exhibit when they find out that they are being taken over before the official announcement is made.

Chapter 1 6.00 p.m., Tuesday, 24 December

People who have worked for a company for some years establish a level of comfort which is highly resistant to change. A new owner, almost invariably planning to make unwelcome alterations to the way work is accomplished, creates counterproductive waves, often of traumatic proportions. This predisposition by employees is called *resistance to change*. Conversation between Brian Curtis and the other three managers at the division Christmas party demonstrates this comfort level, presaging in varying degrees the resistance they are likely to exhibit to a takeover.

Rumours are typically dismissed as gossip. Nonetheless, there is some evidence in the research literature which suggests that rumours are often quite close to the truth, especially if the message is negative. In fact, organizations sometimes make active use of the *rumour mill* when they want to condition employees to a change. The rumour of an imminent takeover making the rounds at the division Christmas party is universally rejected because the implications are too traumatic to contemplate at such a time and place. However, it lingers in the minds of those who have most to lose should it be true. For example, Tony Johns, Director of Regulatory Affairs in the division, expects his job to be made redundant if the rumoured takeover actually occurs.

Chapter 2 11.30 a.m., Saturday, 28 December

On the surface, it may appear to be in a company's best interests not to tell a workforce that their operation is to be sold until the new owners take over. However, there is increasing empirical support for informing employees as soon as the sale has been consummated on paper. When employees are not told at an early stage, it usually has more to do with attempting to maintain secrecy during the sensitive phase of negotiations than concern about a negative effect on morale.

If the intention of both sellers and buyers is to:

- safeguard the financial interests of employees;
- urge employees not to feel threatened by the change of ownership; and
- lead employees to believe that their long-term career prospects will be enhanced by remaining with their new employer,

there is little justification for keeping the takeover secret.

On the other hand, if the buyers plan to make substantial changes affecting the workforce negatively, they will choose to keep the takeover secret until they physically take control of the operation. They will also typically take deceptive measures until they are ready to initiate the changes.

Nevertheless it is almost impossible to keep secret anything of consequence, as "leaked reports" to the media remind us from time to time. The *informal communication system* is a powerful medium for disseminating information, and its effectiveness is well documented in the research literature. For example, in the novel, a secretary inadvertently mentions sighting documents about the takeover. Brian Curtis penetrates the veil of secrecy by phoning a reliable source in the acquiring corporation, confirming the takeover. In the next chapter, the takeover is mentioned to an employee by a bank manager concerned about a home loan.

The informal communication system is an important factor which must be included in the decision-making process when a buyer examines the available options, and it adds weight to the argument for being as open as possible at all times.

A number of views and experiences are discussed about the reasons for takeovers and the impact they have on the employees of the organization being acquired. What emerges is the notion of *equifinality*: that is, there are almost always a number of ways of doing anything. Which method is used depends on an infinite variety of motivations and circumstances operating at the time. Two observations can be elicited from that discussion between the four managers:

1. The success of a takeover is inextricably linked to the level of commitment top decision-makers have to the continuing welfare of their employees.
2. It is in the buyer's best interests to be scrupulously fair and open in its dealings with employees. It takes a long time to create a motivated workforce; it takes no time at all to destroy morale.

The term *high involvement workforce* is mentioned for the first time in the novel. It recurs throughout the book and describes the integration of a company's workforce within a win-win work ethic. The term *mimimax principle* is also mentioned. It does not recur in the book, but it is worth remembering. It is the negative behaviour many employees exhibit when they are not part of a *high involvement workforce.*

Chapter 3 10.30 p.m., Tuesday, 31 December

The prospect of a takeover is never far from the thoughts of employees, even in the concluding moments of an enjoyable New Year's Eve dinner party. The four managers and their wives/partner explore:

- *Different scenarios for the announcement of the takeover.* These run from a full and open disclosure of future plans at a mass meeting of new employees, to intense secrecy and deception, with no meetings and no advance notice of impending changes.
- *Possible reactions of disaffected employees to the takeover.* These can be quite extreme, ranging from altering to damaging, stealing, even destroying irreplaceable physical and intellectual assets. For example, erasing all debtor files from the central computer.
- *Positive initiatives by a new owner.* All need not be "doom and gloom". New owners are almost always conscious of the value of the acquired workforce. Many go to considerable lengths to assimilate them into the mainstream of their activities and culture. Where retrenchments are made, it is often with great sensitivity.

Part II Announcements

Part II is concerned with the impact a takeover has on the employees of an organization when they first conclude that it is not a rumour but a certainty. It also explores the different approaches that can be taken to inform employees officially that their organization has been taken over.

Chapter 4 7.00 a.m., Thursday, 2 January

This chapter deals with each of the four managers as they prepare to return to work after their Christmas holidays. Knowing that the takeover is a certainty, they respond to this event in quite different ways:

- **Britt Berghoff** begins to think about resigning her position and going into business with her live-in boyfriend.
- **Tony Johns** decides he is not going to let the possibility that his job may become redundant affect him adversely. He is going to show the world that he still has much to contribute, despite his age.
- **Armand Hernier** finds the whole business depressing, especially having to conceal the takeover from his colleagues, many of whom may be seriously affected.
- **Brian Curtis** arrives at work early as usual. He is confronted by a subordinate who has been informed by her bank manager that the division has been sold to H & H. She is worried that she will lose her job and her new home, since she is the sole income earner. He has to pretend that he knows nothing definite about the takeover, reassuring that subordinate that her job is secure. His secretary knows him too well and accuses him of dissembling. He continues to pretend that he has no specific information, having committed his friends to maintaining silence, whatever the circumstances. He must do everything he can not to

compromise his source who, after all, may be his future boss. His secretary storms off in disgust.

The purpose of this chapter is to illustrate how differently people respond to an event as traumatic as a takeover. Some will be worried, some will be angry, some will see this as an opportunity to reorganize their lives, some will want to wait and see what happens. But everyone will be concerned and ready to jump in any number of directions, many undesirable, making it difficult for a new owner to benefit fully from the acquisition. For example, "the brightest and the best" have little difficulty in finding alternative employment. With no loyalty to the new employer, they take the opportunity to leave and improve their career prospects.

Chapter 5 4.00 p.m., Thursday, 2 January

There is some evidence, mostly anecdotal, that people, faced with a situation which may have important consequences, tend to display their most desirable characteristics. For example, soldiers stand straighter when officers are in the vicinity, employees are on their best behaviour when they want to impress their superiors, school children pay greater attention when there is an important visitor in their classroom, workers apply themselves more diligently when being inspected by senior managers.

Contrary to his expectations that employees would be standing around discussing the rumoured takeover and the implications of the assembling of a giant marquee on the front lawn of their building, Brian Curtis observes everyone with their heads down, pretending to be hard at work. Like everyone in the building, he also decides he will get back to his desk and pretend to be hard at work. After all, when the axe is likely to be wielded, it doesn't do to stick your head out any further than absolutely necessary!

Chapter 6 7.00 a.m., Friday, 3 January

Brian Curtis visits the fully assembled marquee on his way in to work and is impressed by its size and intricate construction. The marquee leads him to draw the parallel between the forthcoming announcement and a circus act. He envisages each person in the official party putting on a show for the audience, with appropriate dazzle and sleight of hand, like experienced circus performers, ultimately sending the employees of the division home for the weekend feeling good about the future but none the wiser about their prospects.

He chances to meet his old friend, Paul Ruffin, who is inspecting the marquee to see that everything is in order. Paul tells him that he will be the incoming general manager of the division. They discuss briefly the quite different approaches of their two companies to informing employees about the takeover. Although they part on the best of terms, they obviously don't share the same view of their future relationship.

Chapter 7 4.00 p.m., Friday, 3 January

This chapter attempts to capture the atmosphere of the mass meeting, charged with expectations of well-rehearsed messages from a group of highly experienced professionals. Reference to the circus is continued as the speakers process to the stage, led by the chairman of AgriBus. The method used to announce the takeover turns out to be a mixture of "let's do the right thing by our people and make it look good", an expensive stab at conscience-salving, and an attempt to convince the employees that: "There's nothing to worry about, you have everything to gain. In the meantime, it's business as usual."

Chapter 8 3.30 p.m., Sunday, 5 January

The four managers and their wives/partner gather at a home barbecue and attempt to analyse what was said at the Friday afternoon meeting in the marquee. Their intentions are to understand more clearly what may be in store for the division and, indirectly, for each of them. This activity is most probably also going on in the homes of all division employees as they try to divine their future. Their discussion reveals three areas of interest:

1. The reasons for the sale of the division by AgriBus, and the reasons for the purchase of the division by Helm & Hathaway.
2. The characteristics of H & H as an employer.
3. The future course of events as it might affect each of them.

They agree that the various official speakers were sufficiently adept not to reveal any plans which might impact their audience negatively. The emphasis of the meeting, judged from each speaker's remarks, was consistently on the positive aspects of the takeover, as follows:

- They were joining an organization which was large, progressive, and fully appreciated the importance of their most important asset – people.
- The organization was in the human ethicals business. They would now receive the kind of support they needed to achieve their professional objectives and personal ambitions.
- The new owners wanted things to continue as they were. If change was needed, it would be mild and directed at achieving only a slightly different focus.

The conclusion the friends reach is to "have a quiet look around and see what jobs are out there, just in case . . . If we find something, we make our move. Then it's up to H & H to reveal what they have in mind for each of us. We can bargain from a position of strength if we want to stay."

Part III Changes at the top

Part III shows what a new chief executive should do to establish his credentials in his organization. Each new meeting with subordinates, whatever the circumstances, provides an opportunity for him to imprint his management style.

Chapter 9 10.00 a.m., Monday, 6 January

The question addressed in this chapter is how best the new general manager should present himself at a meeting of all the supervisory staff of the division in order to make a favourable impression, and at the same time attempt to convey some implicit messages about his managerial style. The following are some useful techniques used by Paul Ruffin, the incoming general manager:

- It is important to be punctual. Paul Ruffin enters as the clock strikes ten thereby indicating that meetings start promptly at the appointed time. Arriving late for his meetings is not acceptable behaviour.
- It is a good tactic to start the meeting by identifying a grievance and resolving it immediately. His opening statement informs the meeting that the offending pictures of past chairmen on the boardroom walls must go as soon as that can be arranged. This draws the necessary laughs and breaks the ice. It suggests that, unlike Norman Coles, he has a sense of humour, is approachable, and intends to use the authority of his position in their best interests. At the end of the meeting, he reminds his executives that the boardroom is once again available for meetings. In so doing, he relinquishes the proprietory rights of his predecessor, a source of constant irritation for these executives.
- It is important to encourage questions at any stage of that first meeting, even if, on occasion, it interrupts the flow of

ideas and leads to the discussion of topics of peripheral interest. More importantly, all questions should be answered as truthfully as possible. It is preferable to admit ignorance than to attempt to find an answer which is incomplete, incorrect or, worst of all, a lie.

- The audience must come away from this meeting feeling that their new chief executive is not only knowledgeable about the business they're in, but also understands the difficulties associated with takeovers, even admitting that there may have to be a rationalization of employees down the road.
- Providing them with specific instructions about their responsibilities is mandatory. There can be no ambiguity about what is expected of them.

Chapter 10 3.00 p.m., Friday, 10 January

This is Paul Ruffin's first formal meeting with the senior executives who report directly to him. It is imperative that he should imprint his leadership style clearly and firmly at that meeting by conveying the following:

- He is aware that the leadership function involves delegating responsibilities. At the same time, it does not imply his abdication of these responsibilities. In making arbitrary choices of understudies for the heads of departments, Paul Ruffin tells them in no uncertain terms that he is prepared to make decisions which they may have difficulty accepting. There are occasions when he has to make decisions alone, and this is one of them, for better or for worse. In the process, he acquaints them with an important human resource principle: the need to have in place a designated and well-trained second-in-charge for every key position. The way the military organize their command structure is the most obvious example of that principle.
- He creates the **Operating Committee**, the executives who

report directly to him. Its information-sharing function is a critical requirement for any organization. At that most senior level, there is a vital need to communicate downward, upward and laterally on a regular basis, with absolute freedom of expression.

There are three features of his organization which he must attempt to understand quickly. The most efficient method of achieving this objective is to instruct his executives to provide him with that information as soon as practicable, as follows:

1. *What has been achieved in the past and what is planned (forecast) for the future*. The length of that period (looking backwards and forwards) will depend on the nature of the goods and/or services provided by the enterprise. For example, Paul Ruffin is satisfied with a backward look of twelve months and a forward look of six months.
2. *The formal communication mechanisms by means of which things get done*. This includes flow charts of all documentation, records, regular meetings and reports – in effect, any and all the methods by which the enterprise keeps itself informed about its day-to-day activities. This applies to both internal and external connections, such as suppliers and customers.
3. *An assessment of the value of every employee to the organization*. This can be done with some objectivity by developing a set of weighted criteria – a *criticality scale*, against which every employee is measured. Armed with this information, Paul Ruffin explains that he will be able to conduct with greater sensitivity the reduction in the workforce which must follow. This is the first clear indication which the senior executives of the former AgriBus division receive that some employees will be discharged in due course.

Chapter 11 11.45 a.m., Wednesday, 15 January

This chapter illustrates how easily organizations can lose "the brightest and the best", thereby reducing the net worth of the new acquisition from a human asset perspective. Amanda Fowler, the designated second-in-charge of the Research Department, accepts an excellent job offer from another pharmaceutical company.

It is also the occasion when the first of the department heads is offered a "golden parachute", which he accepts. Karl Helmreich, head of the Research Department, decides that the changed parameters of his job make it advisable to leave on favourable terms. However, this event does not necessarily support the popular belief that new CEOs typically choose to surround themselves with their own team.

Chapter 12 3.00 p.m., Friday, 17 January

The immediate impact of the takeover on personnel is discussed at the **Operating Committee**. A number of inferences can be drawn:

- The predictable haemorrhaging of "the brightest and the best" in all three departments of the division occurs. A few of the resignations are completely unexpected and quite damaging to the effectiveness of the operation.
- The experiences that each of the department heads has with exit interviews of "the brightest and the best" suggests that their value or otherwise depends almost completely on the personal styles of these individuals. Where there is considerable confidence and trust in a department head, alternative job opportunities are openly discussed and, if appropriate, the employees are encouraged to go, as in the case of Amanda Fowler. Where a department head is reputed not to be objective and impartial, the exit interview is a for-

mality which produces little insight into the reasons why that individual is resigning.

- The *criticality scale* is found to be extremely useful in focusing an executive's attention on the quality of employees under his or her control. It is suggested that a review of the value of each employee, using the *criticality scale*, should be carried out every six months. In addition, it opens up the possibility that an executive may be as much to blame as the employee if that employee registers low scores on the scale.
- Reference is made to the importance of finding and doing everything possible to retain women who have the potential for promotion to executive ranks.
- The requirement for free and open debate on any issue in the Operating Committee is emphasized. It draws attention to the need for the chairman/chief executive officer to be seen to perform effectively. In fact, "it's far more important for me to perform as your boss than it is for you to perform as my subordinates. If you don't think I'm making it, I have far greater problems than if you aren't making it."

Discussion of the reasons for the haemorrhaging of "the brightest and the best" leads to the formation of a **Communications Committee**. It is composed of individuals who are most knowledgeable about the informal communication system that exists in the organization. The function of the committee is to agree upon methods for advising employees about events that are likely to impact them. Formal communication is mostly through two channels, as follows:

1. Much more MBWA (*managing by walking about*) by Paul Ruffin. This stresses face-to-face meetings with small groups of employees who want information from "the horse's mouth", and the opportunity to ask questions directly.
2. A great deal more written communication – memos, newsletters, notices, posters – prepared by an experienced public relations expert/consultant for maximum effect.

Chapter 13 2.30 p.m., Sunday, 26 January

No matter what situation senior executives find themselves in – for example, a supposedly relaxed barbecue among colleagues and wives – work is never far from their minds. Left alone together for a while, Paul Ruffin attempts to understand what motivates Armand Hernier. He recognizes the significant contribution Armand could make to any research project, but has trouble in deciding what is inhibiting such a performance.

Paul Ruffin forgets for a while the old dictum that "if you work in the East, you do your courting in the West". He remembers in time not to break that dictum and make a serious mistake, professionally and personally.

Part IV Changes everywhere

Part IV deals with the reduction in workforce and the negative impact this has on the personnel side of the organization. It also presages the creation of a *high involvement workforce*, the "whoopee!" workforce that will make it possible for the division to achieve its objectives.

Chapter 14 3.00 p.m., Friday, 1 February

The question addressed in this chapter is how Paul Ruffin can best inform a senior management group that they face an arbitrary reduction in force which will decimate the Marketing Department, as well as a good number of technical and scientific employees over the age of fifty. As he explains it to his Operating Committee, there are a number of compelling arguments for this sudden and completely unexpected action by head office, as follows:

- The nature of the industry is changing. The traditional strength of H & H is in OTC drugs. Its market share in OTC is being eroded by a variety of increasingly aggressive competitors. H & H must restructure its disparate and varied prescription drug operations if it is to continue to grow and prosper. That entails a considerable financial commitment, of which the AgriBus prescription drug division is only one small piece.
- One of the major decisions is to spin off the prescription drug business into a separate company. This requires setting up a completely new marketing operation. It also involves the development of a new and highly focused research programme which will produce the new drugs, and the profits to go with them, and will justify the enormous expense and risks inherent in the industry.

Paul Ruffin explains the manner in which the people on the list will be discharged:

- He proposes to interview each of them and make sure that they understand the full extent of their redundancy entitlements, and then have them escorted off the division premises.
- A highly competent firm of outplacement consultants has been retained to assist the former employees find suitable employment.

He concludes the subject of the reduction in the workforce by reminding the members of the Operating Committee that they must treat the list of people being made redundant as highly confidential. He leaves the list with them, indicating that he trusts them to do the right thing by him, by their positions, and by their colleagues.

Chapter 15 1.00 p.m., Tuesday, 19 February

The three wives of the executives meet for their customary monthly lunch. Gloria Johns, whose husband Tony has been made redundant, expresses her anger. She describes to her two friends his behaviour at home now that he is unemployed. He is demonstrating the extreme depression of a person who has been forcibly retired at a stage in his life when he still has an enormous contribution to make to his profession. In addition, he is convinced he won't find another job, because of his reputation as an uncompromising stickler for the legal requirements of the industry, and because of his age.

Chapter 16 8.15 p.m., Friday, 1 March

Britt Berghoff is having an evening at home with Ron, her live-in boyfriend. They discuss a number of subjects which illustrate the low morale in the division and the impact this is having on everyone there:

- She describes the atmosphere at work as being "like a cemetery". Everyone appears to have lost a colleague and, in many instances, a close friend, and people are spending a great deal of time recounting to each other the psychological and social problems their former workmates are having. In the meantime, they all wait for the next round of firings and apply furiously for other positions, even though their jobs with H & H may be completely secure.
- At the personal level, she thinks she may have been a scientist too long and it's time for a change. A check with the Human Resource Department has revealed that she is entitled to a considerable severance package if she resigns – enough, in fact, to start a new business.

Britt and Ron discuss their proposed business venture and decide that this is as good a time as any to make the break. They will invite their close friends to dinner and see what they think, before taking further steps.

Chapter 17 10.45 p.m., Saturday, 2 March

During dinner, the eight of them discuss Britt and Ron's proposed business venture and agree that it has excellent potential for success.

Their next subject concerns the experiences Tony is having with the outplacement consultants, which he relates as follows:

- First, he explains how devastating he found the first few days of unemployment. "There is nothing more soul destroying for a man who has worked all his life than suddenly to find himself out of a job."
- In an unexpected defence of Paul Ruffin, he recounts what happened at the interview in which Paul informed him that he no longer had a job. It was, he maintains, conducted in a highly professional manner on Paul's part, and with great objectivity.
- He goes on to tell them about the wonderful support he received from Gloria when he was in the depths of despondency. He can't imagine what he would have done without her.
- He then describes the physical layout of the outplacement consultancy, the impressive resources made available to every former employee, the mental discipline and orientation required of him to obtain suitable employment, and the training in a wide range of skills needed to find a job.

They all agree that it must be costing H & H a great deal to make the consultancy service available, and also that without it Tony's chances of finding employment would be severely diminished. The consensus of opinion round the dinner table is that Paul Ruffin and H & H are doing their best to make the redundancies as painless as possible.

Chapter 18 11.00 a.m., Monday, 16 March

The weekly Communications Committee meeting in Paul Ruffin's office deals with the following issues:

- The list of employees who are going to be invited to join H & H on a permanent basis. These consist of the remainder of the employees from the former AgriBus Human Ethicals Division, those who have transferred or are in the process of transferring from other H & H locations, and those who have been recruited from other companies. It excludes employees who have resigned but will leave no later than the end of that month.
- The sooner the employees on the list are advised that they have jobs for at least the remainder of the year, and possibly for as long as they want them, the sooner they can stop spending valuable time looking over their shoulders, and get on with their jobs.
- Paul Ruffin begins to break down his colleagues' resistance to having access to confidential information about the workforce. The list contains not only the names of all the permanent employees, but also their positions and salaries, including his own. This knowledge makes the other members of the committee uncomfortable.
- Paul wants to introduce a programme which will make employees in the division look forward to coming to work every day. He hopes that they will begin to think on Sunday nights, "Whoopee, tomorrow's Monday, I'm going back to work". He receives no help from the members of his committee, however, simply because they have no idea how to achieve this.
- He reduces the size of the problem by proposing they should try and devise a public relations programme which will let employees know that they now have job security. That suggestion is rejected by the others because it is only one

piece of a total package which must be transmitted to the workforce if they are to achieve their objective.

- The suggestion is made that Paul should seek professional help from the Human Resource Department at H & H head office on how to institute such a change programme. He is reminded that he must personally take charge of whatever initiative is proposed and not allow the head office experts to have control of the change process.
- Paul Ruffin ends the meeting by altering the parameters of the communications committee. He wants the existing group to assist him with whatever change programme is finally introduced.

Part V A new beginning

Part V covers the remainder of the year during which the business of creating the *high involvement workforce* is carried out. It describes the implementation of many of the key pieces of the change model and justifies the need seemingly to be ruthless at the early stages of the takeover. It ends the novel on a high note: namely, that the reconstituted division, and everyone in it, are poised to make a truly worthwhile contribution to H & H's human ethicals company.

Chapter 19 11.45 a.m., Monday, 18 May

The Communications Committee meeting covers a variety of Human Resource activities:

- The head office consultant has completed his work advising Paul Ruffin and members of that Committee on what is needed to create a *high involvement workforce*.
- Ingrid Andersen has been appointed Human Resource manager and is the focal point of the change programme.
- The five-stage *team development exercise* has begun with the

preparation of position descriptions for all senior management. Ingrid Andersen is about to start on the next level of supervisory personnel, as well as undertaking stage two of the exercise for senior management.

- The **Advisory Committee**, consisting of elected members from all large sections in the division, is not working as intended. Paul Ruffin reports that he is communicating downward, but that there has effectively been no upward communication during the first two monthly meetings. He wonders what he should do. The short answer is that he expects too much too soon. He has to be patient. Many pieces of the change programme have yet to be put on the table, let alone in place.
- Frustrated, Paul asks what has been achieved so far towards the creation of a *high involvement workforce. The change model*, on which the programme is based, is studied carefully. In fact, a great deal has been achieved. However, he is reminded that the nine characteristics of the model must function interactively if they are to produce the anticipated synergy.
- What is most noticeable about the meeting is the easy flow of discussion, with little regard to differences in rank and authority. Paul Ruffin has worked hard to break down these barriers and misses no opportunity to encourage a team spirit.

Chapter 20 1.00 p.m., Tuesday, 22 July

Lunch at a restaurant for the four friends reveals the changes that have occurred for "the winners and the losers" as a result of the takeover:

- *Gretl Curtis* The promotion of Brian Curtis to head of the Development Department includes the considerable perks of office for a senior executive: first-class travel, five-star hotels, expensive restaurants, national and international

conferences, the pick of training seminars. The travel perks extend to Gretl also if she chooses to accompany him. However, a sixty- to seventy-hour week is normal for Brian Curtis. Notwithstanding, he now thoroughly enjoys his job.
- *Michelle Hernier* The promotion of Armand Hernier to head of the Research Department includes the same perks of office as Brian Curtis, which Michelle also enjoys. Armand puts in long hours as well but he too enjoys his job as never before.

Both women agree that Paul Ruffin has made all the difference. "That's what it takes to get people up and running; a good boss who's excited about the work they are doing, and who treats his people well."

In addition to the perks of high office, the various human resource initiatives are producing a work environment with high morale and much better output. In particular, they discuss the five-stage *team development exercise* which appears to have improved teamwork immeasurably.

They are joined by their other two friends who are late:

- *Britt Berghoff* Her business venture with Ron is prospering and she is very happy. Ron has insisted that she take the day off, buy herself an expensive outfit, and enjoy a leisurely lunch with her friends.
- *Gloria Johns* She explains that she was late because Tony was having one of his bad days. He has still not found a job, and has given up looking. He sits in front of the television all day and glares at anyone who disturbs him. Despite an offer by Britt that he should come and work with her and Ron in their business, Gloria insists that finding a job is something he must do for himself. He is not a person to accept favours.

Chapter 21 10.30 p.m., Friday, 7 November

An official visit by Holman B. Andrews, Paul Ruffin's boss and president of the new prescription drug company, prompts the first dinner party the Ruffins have. Brian and Gretl, and Armand and Michelle are the other dinner guests. It is not only an occasion when Mary Ruffin can show off their expensive home with a suitably magnificent dinner, it is predictably an event where a number of business-related topics are discussed:

- Holman Andrews remarks to Mary that Paul is doing a magnificent job. He compliments Paul on his choice of lieutenants.
- He congratulates himself for encouraging Carla Nielson to accept a position in another company where she is apparently a disaster as a manager. He reminds the others a good scientist is not necessarily a good manager.
- In toasting the three divisional managers, he draws their attention to the possibility that they may have some good news in the very near future, "when all sorts of good things will descend on you and yours . . ."
- Unexpectedly, Armand points out that their excellent performance is due to Paul's outstanding leadership. Brian supports that statement by describing instances associated with Paul's success in creating the immensely desirable *high involvement workforce*.

This reinforces Andrews's assertion that the best managers are people who can pick square pegs and put them in square holes. It also bears out his provocative statement that Paul wasn't selected for the job because Mary throws a wonderful dinner party. "In all fairness, it helps enormously for a man to have a clever wife and superb hostess by his side. But when the chips are down, a man has to prove himself at the workface, not over dinner and drinks."

Chapter 22 3.50 p.m., Thursday, 11 December

The last meeting of the Advisory Committee for the year takes place for the first time in the new Human Resources Centre, a former locker room in the basement of the building. Ingrid Andersen has repainted and equipped that room with discarded furniture from around the building. The attractive transformation is applauded by all the members of the committee, including Paul Ruffin.

The usual agenda is set aside in order to try and determine the progress of the change programme, that is, the creation of a *high involvement workforce*. *The change model* is examined in some depth. Another model, describing an *effective human organization*, provides additional insights into the change process. The following issues are identified:

- Discussion of the profit-sharing scheme under consideration by head office emphasizes the need to distribute the amount set aside for employees equally between all of them. Later on in the meeting, attention is drawn to the much wider meaning of *equitable reward sharing*, which includes share ownership.
- Doubt is cast on the effectiveness of training in *Leadership*. In comparing this activity with the *team development exercise*, there is strong support for discontinuing training in that subject, in favour of *team development exercise* which has much greater on-the-job application.
- A lengthy discussion on the merits of having a Human Resource Department identifies the many and varied tasks carried out by that function. There is general agreement that Ingrid Andersen is doing an excellent job, and the Human Resource Department has a very real contribution to make to the creation and maintenance of a *High Involvement Workforce*.
- There is no way anyone can guarantee *job security*. Too many intangibles are involved. However, Paul Ruffin reassures the

elected members of the committee that, so long as he is in charge of the division, he will do everything he can to safeguard their jobs.

- *Information sharing processes* and *employee participation* are identified as widespread in the developing culture. There is abundant evidence of this through the various committees, regular employee meetings, work teams and informational devices in operation.

Interspersed in the discussion, the following examples are given which highlight the emergence of a *high involvement workforce*:

1. The initiative taken by Ingrid Andersen in equipping her Centre with disused furniture shows how money can be saved and profit increased.
2. Paul Ruffin's approval for the purchase of a lounge suite for the HR Centre shows how rapidly decisions are made in the new culture. Such a request would have taken months to process in a traditional organization, if indeed it was ever authorized.
3. The Christmas party is cancelled with overwhelming support because it is money which can be included in the profit share and spent by employees on activities of their own choosing.

The consensus of opinion in the Advisory Committee is that they now have what amounts to a *high involvement workforce*. A cautionary note is sounded regarding the need constantly to reinforce and maintain the new work culture.

Chapter 23 9.30 a.m., Sunday, 28 December

This last chapter deals with a number of unresolved issues. The four friends and wives/partner are back at the beach house for the Christmas holidays. Unlike the previous occasion a year ago when they faced the takeover of their division, this holiday is tinged with bittersweet farewells and memories, as well as hopes for a productive year ahead:

- They bid farewell to **Tony** and **Gloria Johns** who are moving away. Tony is taking up a position with a legal firm which has a department that specializes in the pharmaceutical industry.
- **Britt (Beebee) Berghoff** and **Ron** are doing very well in their business venture and looking forward to much improved circumstances.
- **Brian Curtis** is now permanent head of the Development Department and is completely satisfied with the changes in his work situation.
- So is **Armand Hernier** who has also been promoted to permanent head of the Research Department and is loving it.

Everything seems to have worked out for the better after all. In reflecting on the year that has just gone by:

- They discuss Paul Ruffin's anonymous arrangement of Tony's job with the legal firm. In spite of this highly desirable initiative, they agree he is "a cold fish . . . completely single-minded and opportunistic . . . with a devious mind". However, they also agree "he's doing one hell of a great job as Division General Manager, and he's a damn good boss". The point that is being made is that it is not necessary for an executive (a leader) to be popular and admired (charismatic) in order to be effective.
- Brian shares with Armand and Ron the concerns he had, back in February, that everyone in the division would be fired and a whole new workforce hired. He explains that it is sometimes more economical to start with a clean slate than try to merge different and quite often antagonistic workforces together. Among other factors, this accounts for Paul Ruffin's need to undertake the complex task of creating

> a *high involvement workforce*, "not because he loves people . . . but because it's just plain good business".

They go over the reasons why a veterinary organization like AgriBus could not be successful in the human ethicals business. These reasons clarify why Brian and Armand believe they will be much better off working for H & H.